Reading Detectives 17ª Aug 2014

Kerry Renshaw grew up in London and studied history at Oxford. He has taught history for many years at different levels, in England and abroad. The idea for this book comes from his fond memories of the News Chronicle I-Spy series, especially 'I-Spy The Sights Of London', which showed him as a child how much hidden history is to be found on the streets of our towns and cities.

If you want to read more about the history you've uncovered
in *Reading Detectives* you'll find it in these books,
also published by Two Rivers Press:

Fox Talbot & the Reading Establishment by Martin Andrews
All Change at Reading: The Railway and the Station 1840–2013
    by Adam Sowan
Caversham Court Gardens: A Heritage Guide by Friends of
    Caversham Court Gardens
Believing in Reading: Our Places of Worship by Adam Sowan
The Reading Quiz Book by Adam Sowan
Broad Street Chapel & The Origins Of Dissent In Reading by Geoff Sawers
Bikes, Balls & Biscuitmen: Our Sporting Life by Tim Crooks
    with Reading Museum
Bizarre Berkshire: An A–Z Guide by Duncan Mackay
Down by the River: The Thames and Kennet in Reading by Gillian Clark
A Mark of Affection by Adam Sowan
The Holy Brook by Adam Sowan
Abattoirs Road to Zinzan Street by Adam Sowan

Reading
Detectives

Kerry Renshaw

With photographs by Electra Colios

TWO
RIVERS
PRESS

First published in the UK in 2014 by Two Rivers Press

7 Denmark Road, Reading RG1 5PA
www.tworiverspress.com

ISBN 978-1-909747-02-9

1 2 3 4 5 6 7 8 9

Two Rivers Press is represented in the UK by Inpress Ltd and distributed by Central Books.

Text design by Rachel Becker and typeset in Parisine.
Trail maps by Geoff Sawers.

Printed and bound in Great Britain by Ashford Colour Press, Gosport.

Two Rivers Press gratefully acknowledges financial assistance from The Earley Charity.

The Earley Charity

by hook or by crook

Foreword

When people walk into town for chips and a drink or whatever, they don't usually notice much. They're too busy nattering to their mates, listening to their music, or thinking about some daft thing they've seen online; anything to shut out the boredom of the journey itself.

They probably look left and right when they cross the road to make sure they don't get squished by a white van, but for the rest of the walk, the whole town could be sprayed jet-black or painted with rainbow-coloured stripes, and they wouldn't spot anything unusual.

But not everyone's like that. Detectives almost always have their eyes wide open searching for clues to help them solve the latest crime. And there are other people who do pretty much the same. I call them history detectives. Wherever they go, in towns and cities throughout the UK, they peer up alleyways and round corners, up church towers and down basements, looking for clues about stories from the past.

And now, thanks to this fantastic book, you can be one too. Yes, right here in Reading, you can become a brilliant detective.

So go on then! Stop reading this boring introduction! Get out there, and start detecting!

Tony Robinson

Acknowledgements

The idea for this book came from conversations with Electra Colios, and her ideas and encouragement have been crucial throughout its preparation. She also took most of the photographs. The children of Alfred Sutton School helped Electra to trial the material, and their enjoyment of it was very heartening. Thanks are due to Val Preston, Headmistress, and to Liz Carpenter, a former teacher at the school.

Adam Sowan is a local historian of renown, and he gave his time, tactfully, courteously and unstintingly to save me from innumerable embarrassments and factual inaccuracies. Any remaining are entirely mine.

Brendan Carr of Reading Museum talked over issues with me and gave invaluable leads to materials, and Margaret Simons, another local historian, pointed out landmarks in the town of which I was entirely ignorant. Ann Smith and Katie Amos at Reading Library and Angela Houghton at the Museum were very helpful with photographs.

The Earley Charity gave a generous grant to help with publication costs, which made all the difference. Rachel Becker prepared excellent designs which inspired us to believe the book would become a reality, but its real midwife is Sally Mortimore of Two Rivers Press, who saw the point of it all right at the outset, who kept faith with us through our many doubts and uncertainties and who made it publishable.

Kerry Renshaw

"No town in the south of England hides its attractions more successfully from the visitor"

John Betjeman and John Piper on Reading, from *Murray's Berkshire Architectural Guide*, 1949

Dear Reading Detectives,

It's fun to be a detective. By following the walking trails in this book and answering the questions, you can find out all sorts of interesting facts about people who have lived in and visited Reading over hundreds of years.

Did you know that the engineering genius, Brunel, would have celebrated the coming of the Great Western Railway here in 1840, only a few days after a young workman was tragically hurled to his death by a whirlwind from the new station roof? How did Queen Victoria lose a finger here? And what is the connection, on that very same day, with Paddington Bear? George Palmer – with stone umbrella and baggy trousers – once looked down on huge crowds welcoming the first electric trams to Broad Street, the same street where Queen Elizabeth I frequently stayed.

These things happened long ago but clues to their existence can be discovered by intrepid and dedicated explorers. Good detectives use their eyes to look closely at the buildings, statues, street signs, shop fronts, bridges and rivers and piece together the clues to create a living history of our town.

Detectives don't need to work alone. You'll enjoy looking for clues with friends or family. Walk the trails together and help each other to solve the questions. The extra information we've given you with the answers will help you reconstruct the past so you'll be able to close your eyes and let your imaginations travel back in time. Pictures, sounds and even smells may come to mind from a different time. Around the Forbury Gardens you may see hooded monks on their way to prayers in the magnificent Abbey, or hear the sounds and bloody sights of the execution of the Abbot in 1539. Near St Mary's Butts you might encounter boys practising archery or run into a group of young Danish hostages from the Napoleonic Wars. You might attend Royal funerals, Royal weddings and even Royal births and enjoy a mighty open-air banquet stretching all the way down London Street. You may even sniff the delicious aromas of biscuits baking on King's Road and hops roasting on Bridge Street.

To discover the most hidden clues and secrets of Reading, complete each trail then turn to the answers page for that trail to check that you saw everything and to find out much more about the town around you – murders, mystery and lots of biscuits!

During the planning of this book, a group of children from Alfred Sutton Primary School investigated parts of the trails. They really enjoyed finding the answers to the questions and thought the extra information was really interesting. We would like to thank Samyucthaa, Alyssa, Elsa, Isabella, Dominic, Sammy and Danny for taking part. We hope that you have as much fun as they did.

Remember to keep your eyes peeled!

Happy hunting,
Kerry and Electra

The question trails cover a wide area so if you only have time to walk around the Town Centre, look for the ones marked with this logo: **T.C.**

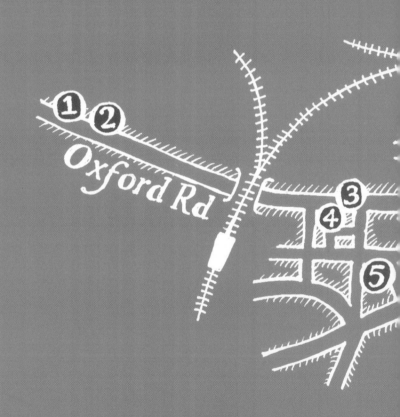

TRAIL 1:
WEST TO EAST

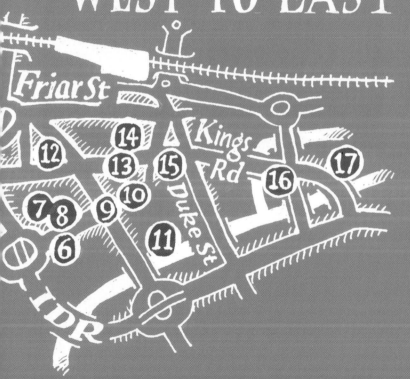

1   Location: Battle Public Library. 420 Oxford Rd, RG30 1EE

Who laid the library's foundation stone?

_____

_____

2   Location: The former Battle Hospital

On the inside wall of this gateway is a memorial plaque to a
soldier who died in the First World War.

What was his name, and on what date did he die?

Who was he?
_____

When did he die?
_____

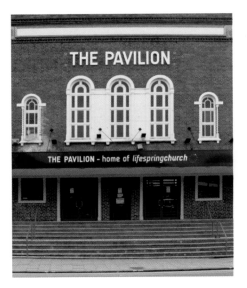

3   Location: The Pavilion Church

This building is now a church, named after a cinema from
the past called The Pavilion. **Look at the back wall of
the building – what you think it was used for
in more recent times?**

_____

_____

_____

4   Location: Goldsmid Road

What is this unusual red-brick building that has an onion shape on its roof?

_____

_____

_____

5   Location: 55 Baker Street

Here was located the workshop of a famous pioneer whose influence spread around the world. **Who was he, when did he work here and of what was he 'the father'?**

Who was he?

_____

When did he work here?

_____

Of what was he 'the father'?

_____

This is actually two photos joined together. Taken between 1844 and 1846, they show Nicolaas Henneman (Fox Talbot's assistant) and, possibly, Talbot himself at work outside their workshop.

6 Location: The Almshouses, Castle Street

This ancient Reading street now contains the police station, several historic buildings, and some attractive little cottages, called The Almshouses, which slope down to the right from Castle Street.

Look at the stone plaque on the wall, to the right of the entrance to the almshouses. **Originally the houses were built as accommodation for poor men, but for how many?**

THE THREE B'S

Bulbs

This is the Suttons garage on The Forbury, with its impressive curved roof and beautifully decorated frontage. The picture dates from about 1905. The space is now occupied by Carluccio's Restaurant and the square in front of it.

Suttons Seeds is a long-established company, producing seeds, bulbs and other products for farmers and gardeners. They were one of Reading's big employers, and were one of the famous 'Three B's' of Reading. Today they are based in Devon, but for many years, from 1806, the company was one of the leading traders in Reading, and helped to make the town famous. They occupied buildings in Market Place, where they had their shop, plus nurseries along Queens Road and stables on The Forbury. From the 1960s they had huge nurseries

READING. FORBURY ROAD.

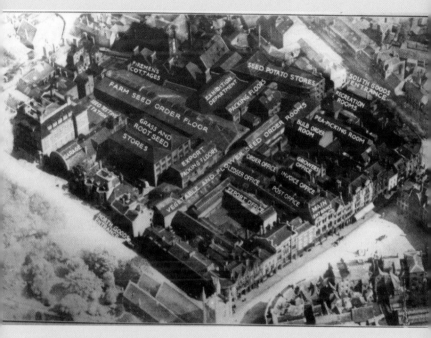

Aerial view of the Suttons Seeds stores and offices. They covered a large area of central Reading. Market Place is the light space on the right hand side, near the bottom. The building labelled 'Garage' is on The Forbury. Notice the company had its own fire brigade! The picture was taken about 1921.

for raising seeds and plants on the land that is now Suttons Business Park in Earley.

Alfred Sutton Primary School is named after a member of the family. Suttons had contributed money to the founding of the school in 1902. For its first 20 years or so it was known as Wokingham Road School, and afterwards as Alfred Sutton. The family also contributed money to Wessex Hall at Reading University.

Biscuits

Huntley & Palmers was probably the best-known company that Reading ever had, and for many years in the 19th and 20th centuries, Reading was famous above all for biscuits – one of the 'Three B's' of beer, bulbs and biscuits. The Reading Football Club was known as the 'Biscuitmen' or the 'Biscuit Boys', as was the Royal Berkshire Regiment.

The business started in the 1820s and their little shop in London Street was the site from 1826. Biscuits would be sold to travellers on the London to Bath stage coaches which stopped at the nearby Crown Inn.

Production continued in London Street until 1861. By then George Palmer had joined the firm and the great factory on King's Road had opened in the 1840s. Only one building of the many on the King's Road site still remains. At one time the factory had 12 miles of its own railway track and locomotives, and the canal ran through the factory complex. It even had its own fire brigade!

The company had 16 workers in 1844, but 50

years later had 5,000 – it was the biggest biscuit manufacturer in the world, covering 24 acres.

The terraced houses of Newtown were built from the 1840s to the 1870s and its closeness to the factory made it an ideal place for the Huntley & Palmers workers to live. Lower Caversham was also a popular area for employees as they could walk to the factory across the Clappers footbridge. Many women and girls worked in the factory, and there are photographs of Votes for Women meetings outside the factory shortly before the First World War.

In its early days the company always bought ingredients from the local area, which helped Berkshire farmers, millers and their labourers. Local transporters such as carters and barge owners relied on work from Huntley & Palmers. Flour came from mills within a few miles of Reading, such as the Sonning Mill or Mapledurham Mill. The old Abbey Mill produced flour for the company up to the 1950s.

Every kind of cake and biscuit was produced in all sorts of packages, tins and boxes for supply to the United Kingdom, India and the rest of the British Empire. Over the years, 400 different kinds of biscuit were produced. As a result, the name of Reading could be found in every corner of the globe, particularly in the British Empire, and even in Tibet and in Antarctica with Captain Scott. The beautifully-decorated Huntley & Palmers biscuit tins were collected and kept for storage in countless households, and some can fetch high prices today. The excellent rail services from Reading, as well as the canal, greatly helped in the trade. First class passengers from London were given free samples of the best biscuits, and were told to look out for the factory as they passed through Reading.

The fame of the factory attracted many notable visitors, including members of the Royal family on several occasions.

The company was always closely involved with the town. In 1875 George Palmer gave 14 acres of King's Meadow, beside the River Thames, for use as a recreation ground. This was followed in 1889 when he gave 49 acres of land in east Reading. The land was planted with trees at George Palmer's expense and became Palmer Park. He also gave land to the University and for local schools.

During the First World War the factory packaged 250,000 tons of basic rations for the armed services.

After the war, the company found trading more difficult, but it continued, helped by merging with other companies such as Peek Frean. After the Second World War it was harder to find enough workers in Reading. The company stopped production in Reading in 1976, but continued to produce biscuits in Liverpool.

Eventually almost the entire site was cleared
and is now occupied by Homebase, Toys R Us,
Staples, Prudential and a number of other firms.

Beer

William Simonds, the son of an old Berkshire
family, opened a small brewery in 1774 on
Broad Street. In 1789 his son, William Blackall
Simonds, opened a new brewhouse at Seven
Bridges, so known because of the many
bridges needed over the shallow channels of
the Kennet. The brewhouse was designed by

This wonderful
steam-driven
delivery engine
and trailer, from
1924, would have
trundled barrels of
Simonds' beer all
over Berkshire in
the 1920s.

the locally-born architect Sir John Soane, who also designed the lighted obelisk in Market Place.

The brewery was greatly expanded in 1895. It covered the area occupied now by House of Fraser, and also over the other side of the river, along Fobney Street, where Loch Fyne and the new apartments now stand. The riverside site was very important: barley for malting came from the west on the River Thames and the Kennet and Avon Canal, and beer was sent to London by barge until the 1930s. The company took water from on-site artesian wells, an important clean source in the days before water treatment. Artesian wells are 'natural' wells where the water rises under its own pressure, and does not have to be pumped.

An old print, from about 1875, of the Simonds Brewery by the Kennet near Bridge Street. Notice the number of towns in which they had offices. They were an international exporter of beer.

LONDON STORES:—12, Millbank Row, S.W.

H. & G. SIMONDS, Pale Ale & Porter Brewers,

WINE AND SPIRIT IMPORTERS, READING.

District Offices and Agencies at
Aldershot, Beckenham, Blackwater, Brighton, Croydon, Dover, Exeter, East Grinstead, Farnborough, Hartley Row, Newbury, Oxford, Red Hill, Sandgate, Slough, Swindon, Twickenham, Woolwich, Wokingham, &c.

Simonds supplied the British Army at home and overseas, and set up breweries and depots abroad. India Pale Ale was a Simonds beer, sold in India when it was part of the British Empire. Huntley & Palmers biscuits were also popular there, so the name of Reading must have popped up frequently on the tables of British soldiers and officials in India.

Between 1910 and 1929 the chairman was George Blackall Simonds, a famous sculptor, who in earlier years had created the Maiwand Lion in Forbury Gardens and the statues of Queen Victoria and George Palmer in Reading.

In February 1943, one of the four bombs that fell on the town centre caused a 25-foot crater on the Simonds site.

By 1953 the company included 1132 pubs, 36 hotels and 80 off-licences across the South of England. In 1960 they merged with Courage Breweries, who left the Severn Bridges/Bridge Street site in 1980 for a new site close to the M4, south of Reading. Courage in turn left there in 2010.

During the many decades that Simonds and Huntley & Palmers were both producing in Reading, the aromas of biscuits baking and beer brewing frequently drifted across the rooftops of the town.

It's a myth !

Many people have thought that Queen Victoria's statue has its back to Reading because she did not like the town.

In fact, there is no record of the Queen ever having visited Reading. It was probably placed here where people would see it welcoming them as they walked up from the station.

7   Location: The Civic Centre

T.C. There is a small, squarish sculpture to the right of the main entrance to the Civic Centre. It is a Spanish Civil War memorial, and it has inscriptions which tell you about Reading people who died in that war. One of them was Archibald Francis. **Can you find out where he died, and when?**

_____

_____

8 Location: Opposite the Civic Centre is a wall depicting cartwheeling boys:

What does it commemorate?

_____

_____

_____

And why are the boys cartwheeling?

_____

_____

_____

9 Location:
St Mary's Butts

Look at the
memorial in the
centre of the road.
On it you will find
an inscription about
a very famous
historical figure, and
a special event in
that person's life.
**What does
the memorial
commemorate,
and in what year
was the event?**

What does the memorial commemorate?

_____

_____

What was the year of the event?

_____

10 Location: St Mary's Church  on St Mary's Butts

The Minster Church of St Mary the Virgin stands in its ancient graveyard. Find the plaque with an inscription on the side wall of this beautiful old church.
Who was the Danish merchant commemorated on the plaque, and how old was he when he died?

Who was the Danish merchant?

_____

_____

How old was he when he died?

_____

11 Location: Bridge Street/Riverside, near The Oracle

T.C. On the south-west side of the canal, opposite the House of Fraser, there is an information panel about the Simonds Brewery.

a) **Where did the company take its water from?**

b) **Which famous man visited the brewery in 1926?**

12 Location: Oxford Road, corner of West Street

At the junction with Oxford Road and Broad Street there is a block of shops opposite you, between West Street and Cheapside.

This used to be a very large department store built in beautiful red brick and tiles. Look carefully at the side of the building on West Street and you can still (just about) see the name of the store. **What was it?**

Did you know ?

The railway to Reading had to be diverted through a hillside.

Brunel was possibly the greatest engineer in British history. He built bridges, railways, tunnels and steamships, and helped make Britain the first industrial nation of the 19th century. He also built the railway bridge over the Kennet, and the famous Sonning Cutting, just east of Reading. The residents of Sonning did not want the noisy, smoky railway to come too close to them, so Brunel had to divert the railway through Sonning Hill, which took two years to excavate and caused the deaths of several workers. The cutting is a mile long and 60 feet deep in places.

13 Location: Waterstone's Bookshop, 89A Broad Street

 Looking above the entrance to the bookshop, **can you tell what this building was in earlier times? Can you find signs of its previous use inside, as well as outside?**

What was the building used for in earlier times?

_____

_____

_____

14 Location: Moss (menswear
    (T.C.) shop), Broad Street

**What animal can you
see above the shop
doorway, close to the
roof? What colour is it?
Why is it there?**

What is the animal?

_____

What colour is it?

_____

Why is it there?

_____

_____

15 Location: The George Hotel, 12 King Street

This is said to be the oldest existing non-religious building in Reading – the Minster Church of St Mary and St Laurence's Church are older – and its origins date back to the 15th century. The hotel has the white plaster and black timbers common to Tudor buildings of that time.

Inside the courtyard of this old coaching inn there is a bar named after a famous author. **Who is the author?**

_____

_____

Did you know **?**

There is a
'Reading power
station' in Tel
Aviv, Israel.

16 Location:
Girl and swan
sculpture,
close to 100
King's Road

**Who created
this sculpture,
and on what
date was it
unveiled?**

Who was the creator?

_____

_____

What was the unveiling date?

_____

_____

17 Location: Huntley & Palmers building, Kings Road

One fairly small red brick building, now converted into apartments, is all that remains of the great Huntley & Palmers factory, once the largest biscuit factory in the world.

The triangular shape at the front of the building, supporting the roof, is called the 'pediment'. This was a common feature in classical architecture, and often imitated in the 18th and 19th centuries in Europe and the USA on important buildings. The Royal Berkshire Hospital also has a pediment.

On the pediment of the Huntley & Palmers building is a date and a sculpture of parts of a plant.
What is the date, and what are the parts of the plant?

What is the date?

_____

What are the plant parts?

_____

_____

Well done for finishing the **West to East trail**, now turn to **page 106** to find out the answers to all the questions and much more!

Why not retrace your steps now as you read about Reading's archery butts, where The Oracle got its name and a very special 'crystal palace'?

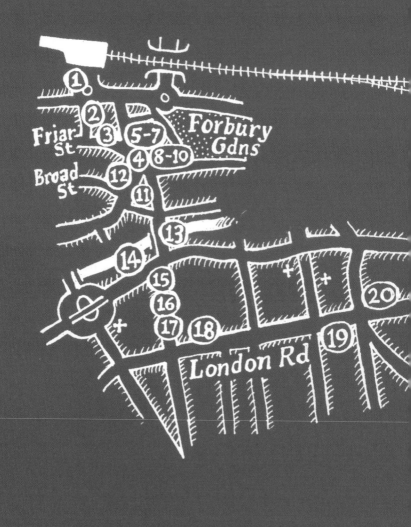

Wokingham Rd

21
22
23
24

TRAIL 2:
NORTH TO EAST

1   Location: Reading Station,

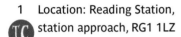

station approach, RG1 1LZ

The statue opposite the station entrance is of an imposing figure standing on a plinth, gazing at the station. It represents a King, **but which King?** The inscription also calls him an Emperor. **Emperor of where? Who donated the statue to Reading?**

Who is the King?

_____

_____

Of where was he Emperor?

_____

Who donated the statue?

_____

2   Location: Malmaison Hotel, 18-20 Station Road

 Which railway company's name is above one of the entrances to the hotel?

Did you know **?**

There are chalk mines underneath Palmer Park.

It is traditional for Carter's Steam Fair to visit Palmer Park every year. However, they stopped in 2001 because it looked like the ground was giving way. Chalk mines were found underneath the park and the weight of the fairground rides posed great danger. The stadium events were also affected. Areas around the park were fenced off to stop people from straying on to ground that might cave in, but these have been shored up and compacted so the ground is now safe. Carter's Fair returned in 2013.

3   Location: Yates's Wine Lodge, Friar Street

T.C. Look at the front of this building, **can you tell what it was before it became Yates's?**

_____

_____

𝒟id you know ?

Reading was once known in every corner of the world for the excellent biscuits baked in the town.

4 **T.C.** Location: Friar Street/ Blagrave Street, near the Town Hall

Here stands the imposing statue of one of Britain's most famous monarchs, Queen Victoria. **Who was Mayor of Reading when it was erected? Can you see anything missing from the Queen?**

Who was Mayor?

_____

_____

What is missing?

_____

_____

5 Location: The Town Hall, Blagrave Street

T.C. The Town Hall is a beautiful red and grey brick building with a clock tower, built in the Gothic revival style – a classic Town Hall of the Victorian era. **What date is inscribed above the entrance under the clock tower?**

The Town Hall is home to Reading Museum where you can discover more about Reading's history (www.readingmuseum.org.uk).

6   **Location: Inside the Town Hall** (This location may not be
accessible to the public during special events and at weekends)

T.C.

On the first floor is a display case. The brown plaque
commemorates a tragic and terrifying event that occurred
in Reading in the middle of the last century.

What was the event and when did it happen?

What was the event?

_____

_____

When did it happen?

_____

_____

7   Location: Inside the Town Hall

 This painting on the first floor shows a ceremony.
**Who are the couple in the centre? In what year,
and where, did the ceremony take place?**

Who are the couple?

_____

_____

What was the year?

_____

Where was the ceremony?

_____

8   Location: St Laurence's Church, The Forbury.

    Look at the drinking fountain at the side of the tower. This would
have been especially useful for poor people who could not afford to
buy a drink. Look at it closely – **when was the fountain built?**
Above the fountain, higher up on the tower, you will see a sundial
with a date. **What is the date?**

When was the fountain built?

_____

What is the date on the sundial?

_____

DE MONTFORT ISLAND

Close to Caversham Bridge, as you look towards Reading Bridge, you will see De Montfort Island, also known as Fry's Island. On 8 April 1163, there was a single combat trial here involving Robert de Montfort and Henry de Essex. Robert had accused Henry of cowardice and treason, and King Henry II ordered them to decide the issue in one-to-one combat. Henry appeared to have been killed in the fight, and Robert was declared the winner.

However, monks carried Henry away on his shield and cared for him in the abbey, where he slowly recovered. Some say he became a Benedictine monk. As a convicted traitor, however, his estates and offices were forfeit and his family disgraced.

De Montfort Road, off Vastern Road, takes its name from Robert, and nearby is De Bohun Road, that being one of the names of the Essex family.

The battle on de Montfort Island. King Henry II is watching the contest. Essex lies defeated and surrendering to de Montfort. Reading Abbey is in the background.

9   Location: St Laurence's Churchyard

T.C. Walk down the little alleyway to the left of the west doors of the
church and you will come to the Henry West memorial. This is a
curved wooden board over one of the graves.

Who was Henry West?

_____

_____

What happened to him, and where?

_____

_____

...gures

...es of three
...ted close to
...ve Childcare
...mall courtyard
...e's Churchyard.
...e is called 'Adam,
...ren'.

P. 41 While this book was being printed it was announced that this site is being redeveloped and the statue has been removed.

...he sculptor, and when was the sculpture made?

...e sculptor?

When was it made?

11 Location: Market Place

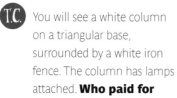

You will see a white column on a triangular base, surrounded by a white iron fence. The column has lamps attached. **Who paid for this structure?**

_____

_____

12 Location: Market Way, Market Place

T.C.

This is the entrance to an arcade of shops.

You can see the lettering above the entrance telling you that this is Market Way, but look for some more lettering higher up.
What was the building originally?

_____

_____

Did you know ?

People could tell the time before clocks were invented.

Sundials are shadow-clocks. Ancient sundials were used for measuring time before clocks were invented, but they continued to be used long after that, and are still made today. A skyscraper in Taiwan is used as a giant sundial to tell the time in an adjoining park.

Early sundials were not always divided into hours – some were divided into three-hour periods called 'tides', as in the expression 'time and tide wait for no man'. The oldest sundial in England is at Bewcastle Cross, Cumbria, dating from the 7th or 8th century. The Ancient Egyptians are thought to have used shadow-clocks about 1,500 years before Christ was born.

13 Location: Duke Street Bridge, also known as High Bridge

T.C. The bridge is made of beautiful honey-coloured stone.
**In what year was it rebuilt by the corporation
(another word for the local council)?**

Did you know **?**

If you had published a
photograph of the bomb
damage at the time of
the raid, you could have
been arrested.

The government didn't want
the Germans to know how
much damage they had done.

This photo shows the extent of the damage in the Town Hall area.
It could only be published some years after it was taken.

14 Location: Mill Lane

 Look up, and you will see lettering in stone which marks the site
of a special place in Reading's transport history.

What form of transport does the lettering refer to?

15 Location: Great Expectations Hotel & Bar. London Street

The building near the bottom of London Street, with its imposing columns, is now the Great Expectations Hotel & Bar. Charles Dickens once gave a reading of his works in this building, and the hotel is named after one of his most famous novels.

If you look just inside the doorway, to the right, you will see some cartoons of Dickens' characters. **Who is the character, shown in a cartoon, who has the same name as a metal?**

16 Location: Addington House, London Street

Look for the blue plaque on the wall. The plaque commemorates
Anthony Addington. **What was his profession, and who was
his famous client? What important job did Addington's
son obtain?**

What was his profession?

_____

Who was his client?

_____

What was his son's job?

_____

Did you know ?

Reading was famous for the 'Biscuit Boys'.

The Royal Berkshire Regiment was nicknamed the 'Biscuit Boys', because of Reading's association with Huntley & Palmers great biscuit factory. Reading Football Club were known by the same nickname for many years.

17 Location: 121 London Street. Huntley House

This looks like an ordinary shop front, but is actually a very historic site for one of Reading's great industries.

There is a round plaque on the wall above the entrance. **What does it commemorate?**

18 Location: Kendrick View, London Road

Next to Kendrick School in London Road there is a very fine
Georgian House called Kendrick View, now occupied by a dentist.
It has a plaque on the wall, telling you that a famous author of the
early 19th century used to live there. **Who was the author, and
which of her books is mentioned?**

Who was the author?

_____

Which books are mentioned?

_____

_____

19 Location: Royal Berkshire Hospital, London Road entrance

This is probably the best known building in Reading, and many local people were born here.

Go up the main steps between the great columns, and in to the entrance hall. Up another short flight of steps, and there is a carved wooden board commemorating the founding of the hospital, with names of notable medical staff who have worked at the Royal Berks.
Who were the first three surgeons at the hospital?

_____

_____

_____

Did you know (**?**)

Broad Street was once the site of a battle.

Broad Street has always been the main shopping street in Reading and in 1688 it was the site of a small but important battle.

King James II was under threat from the invading army of Prince William of Orange, who was moving towards London from the West Country with a force of Dutch and English soldiers, amongst others. William was a Dutchman, married to James' daughter Mary.

James' army was camped on Hounslow Heath, just outside London (where Heathrow airport is now), but he had an advanced guard of 600 Irish soldiers posted in Reading. The Irish people mainly supported James, because he, like most of them, was a Roman Catholic.

These Irish soldiers struck fear into the people of Reading, who asked William for help. He sent 250 of his Dutch troops to clear the Irish out of the town. The walls of St Mary's churchyard were lined with defending Irish musketeers, and a contingent was posted in Broad Street and in the Market Place. But the townspeople warned William's men, and told them where the Irish were positioned, so the Dutch approached from a different direction. They got into the town before the Irish were aware they'd arrived, and attacked them from behind.

James' men were driven down Broad Street and into Market Place, and there they panicked. The whole Irish force fled out of the town towards Twyford. As they did so, townspeople fired on them from upstairs windows.

The Irish lost their flags and fifty of them died. Only about five of the Dutch soldiers were killed. Several of the dead were buried in St Giles' churchyard.

This little battle is known as the 'Reading Skirmish'. Slight as it was, it was the only real conflict in what became known as the Glorious Revolution.

20 Location: King George V
    Gardens, Eldon Square

This is a quiet space for
relaxing, just alongside the
very busy London Road.

You will see the statue of
a Reading MP, Rufus Isaacs
(although his name is not
given on the plinth of
the statue). **What is he
holding in his left hand?**

Did you know **?**

The Duchess of Cambridge and her sister Pippa were born at
the Royal Berks Hospital, though that's not the reason
it's called 'Royal'!

21 Location: Old Reading Cemetery, Cemetery Junction (enter via the arch at the junction)

Towards the back of the cemetery you will see a very lifelike sculpture of a smiling young man – the Hieatt grave.

Bernard Laurence Hieatt died tragically young in an accident in 1930. He was an expert at two forms of ultra-fast travel.

What were the two forms of travel, and how old was he when he died?

What were the forms of travel?

_____

_____

How old was he when he died?

_____

22 **Location: Old Reading Cemetery, Cemetery Junction**

Find the War Memorial in the far right corner of the cemetery, furthest from the entrance.

Some of the soldiers commemorated on the 1914–18 War Memorial belonged to regiments from other countries apart from Great Britain and Ireland. **Can you name two of those other countries?**

_____

_____

23 Location: Palmer Park Gates, Wokingham Road

These impressive gates have stone engravings on the pillars. On the centre pillar are faces, with one wearing a crown. On either side you can see carvings of objects that remind you of the seashore. **What are those objects?**

_____

_____

This statue stood in the middle of Broad Street between 1891 and 1930 when it was moved to Palmer Park.

24 **Location: Palmer Park, Wokingham Road**

George Palmer's statue stands proudly in the middle of the park, and he is clutching his umbrella.

a) The inscription on the statue tells you that George Palmer was 'Member' for the borough, i.e. the Member of Parliament for Reading. **Between what dates was he an MP?**

_____

b) **What important position did he hold in the town of Reading apart from being its MP?**

_____

Well done for completing
the **North to East trail**
through Reading. Why not turn
to **page 118** to find out the
answers to all the questions
and learn more about what
you've seen.

Find out about Reading's links
with Paddington Bear, a visit
from 'The White Queen' and
the famous street party for
6,000 people!

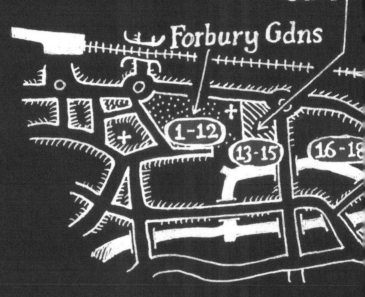

Gasworks Rd

Kenavon Dr

20

9

steps here from Kings Rd
down to Kennetside

TRAIL 3:
The Forbury
and the Abbey

Did you know ❓

'Butts' is an old word for an archery target range.

Many towns in England have an area known as 'The Butts' and Reading has St Mary's Butts.

1 **Location: The entrance to the Forbury Gardens, The Forbury, RG1 3EJ**

The War Memorial is just outside the main entrance to the gardens. Memorials were built in nearly every town in Britain after the First World War to commemorate those who had died in the armed forces. **To whom is this memorial dedicated?**

_____

_____

2   Location: The entrance to the Forbury Gardens, The Forbury

T.C. On the information panel at the main entrance to the gardens, you are told about the company that gave help with the original planting of the gardens. It says that the ground had been in a poor state and the company transformed this 'desert of weeds'.
Which company was it that helped?

_____

_____

3   Location: The Maiwand Lion, Forbury Gardens

T.C. This magnificent beast dominates the gardens and is an icon of Reading. The lion is actually another war memorial to those killed in wars in Afghanistan in the 19th century.

How many Private Smiths are named on the memorial plaques? What other places in Afghanistan, apart from Maiwand, are mentioned on the main plaque?

How many Private Smiths are named?

_____

What other places are named?

_____

_____

_____

4   Location: The *Ilex* tree, Forbury Gardens

 The *Ilex* is a member of the holly family of trees, and 'ilex' is the
Latin name for holly.

The tree stands on its own – **it commemorates the marriage
of which couple and when?**

Who are the couple?
_____

When was the marriage?
_____

5   Location: Forbury Hill, Forbury Gardens

 This mound does not look very significant now, but it is of great interest to historians.

Who directed 'the beautifying of the hill' in 1831?

It's a myth (!)

A story circulated that the lion's sculptor, George Simonds, committed suicide after realising that he had made mistakes in depicting the anatomy of a lion. In fact he had a successful career for many years afterwards, and the lion is anatomically correct!

6 Location: King Henry's Memorial, Forbury Gardens

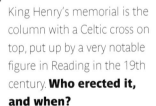

King Henry's memorial is the column with a Celtic cross on top, put up by a very notable figure in Reading in the 19th century. **Who erected it, and when?**

Who erected the column?

_____

_____

When was it erected?

_____

THE FORBURY AND THE ABBEY

7   Location: The Forbury Hotel, The Forbury,

T.C.   facing the Forbury Gardens

This is a fine example of a late Edwardian building. The stone plaque on the side of the building tells you about it.

Who used to occupy it, and when was it built?

Who occupied it?

_____

When was it built?

_____

8   Location: Reading Crown Court, The Forbury

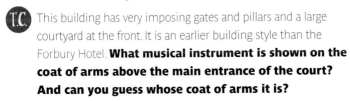

This building has very imposing gates and pillars and a large courtyard at the front. It is an earlier building style than the Forbury Hotel. **What musical instrument is shown on the coat of arms above the main entrance of the court? And can you guess whose coat of arms it is?**

What is the musical instrument?

_____

Whose coat of arms?

_____

THE BRIDGES

The Original Caversham Bridge, 1230s–1869

It occupied more or less the same site on the River Thames as today's bridge – chosen because it was a part of the river where there were several islands to act as natural foundations. This first Caversham Bridge has been described as a great feat of engineering for its time, and was referred to in 1314 as 'The Great Bridge'. It lasted over 400 years until its partial demolition at the time of the Civil War – the people of Reading destroyed it to halt invading troops. This old bridge was partly repaired, and remained in use until 1868. At one time the Oxfordshire half of the bridge was stone, and the Berkshire side wooden! The Chapel of St Anne stood on the medieval bridge, and stones from it were later built into the altar of St Anne's Church, Caversham in the 1950s.

The second Caversham Bridge, 1869–1926

The growth of Reading and the poor state of the existing bridge meant that a new river crossing was essential. The old bridge was demolished, and a new iron bridge was initiated by William Crawshay, the wealthy owner of Caversham Park. This new bridge opened in 1869 and remained in use until 1924.

The present Caversham Bridge, 1926–present

It was opened by the Prince of Wales (later Edward VIII) in 1926. The Prince made a number of visits to places in Reading that day, including Simonds Brewery and Palmer Park. The new bridge was made of ferro-concrete, had two arches and took almost two years to build.

Reading Bridge, 1923–present

This was the second river crossing joining Caversham and Reading and was built in 1923. Traffic had increased greatly as motor cars and lorries became widely used. It had to be built before the old Caversham Bridge was demolished, in order to maintain a river crossing at this site. Reading Bridge was built of the new material, ferro-concrete, and many people were unsure if it would be safe. It was built with one single arch, which also surprised many, but has stood the test of time very well.

Nearby was the site of the treacherous and dangerous old 'Clappers' wooden footbridge across the Thames. The new bridge was especially helpful to people in Lower Caversham, who before had to rely on the Clappers, including those who worked at the Huntley & Palmers factory in King's Road.

A version of the Clappers still exists today, by Caversham Lock. Its name apparently means 'a raised footpath', and, as with Caversham Bridge, the footbridge has ancient origins.

This splendid array of steam-powered vehicles was used to test the strength of Reading Bridge before its opening in 1923.

9   Location: The Abbey Gateway

T.C. This impressive gateway gives you an idea of the location and
appearance of the abbey, even though it has been restored in a
somewhat different style. **Who restored the gateway after it
collapsed in the 1860s? And why did it collapse?**

Who restored it?
_____

Why did it collapse?
_____

10 Location: Information board at the end of Abbot's Walk, in front of the fence and the abbey ruins

T.C.

a) The board attached to the gate shows a painting of the burial of Henry I in 1136. **When was it painted?**

When was it painted?
_____

b) As you look straight ahead you see a stone and flint building that belongs to the nearby St James Church. It is now a day nursery. **What can you see on top of the building that suggests it was once a school?**

_____

Retrace your steps and turn down the service road/path that lies between the houses in this picture and the large office block to find the location for the next question.

THE FORBURY AND THE ABBEY

11 Location: Sculpture near the abbey ruins

In the garden is a sculpture of a robed figure.

Who is the sculptor, and when was the figure created?

Who is the sculptor?

_____

_____

When was it created?

_____

_____

12 Location: Sculpture in the Abbey Gardens, Abbey Street, near the abbey ruins

T.C.

Through the gardens and down the steps at the far end is a sculpture that is a mysterious piece with different shapes. It seems to depict faces breaking out of big stone eggs. The sculptor's name is given on the plinth. **Who is the sculptor, and when was it placed there?**

Who is the sculptor?

_____

_____

When was it placed?

_____

_____

13 Location: Information pillar, Chestnut Walk

T.C. Chestnut Walk runs along the bank of the River Kennet, close to the abbey ruins and Reading Prison. At the start of the Walk, near to the sculptures mentioned above, there is an information pillar that tells you where the abbey wharf was located.

What was the wharf used for?

_____

_____

Did you know (?)

Royalists and Roundheads once fought on Caversham Bridge.

This was probably the most dramatic incident in the bridge's history, when it played a key role in the Civil War and the siege of Reading. The Royalist troops of Charles I were defending the town against the surrounding troops of the Parliament forces (the Roundheads), under the Earl of Essex.

On 25th April, 1643, Colonel Fielding, the Royalist commander, called a truce and began negotiations for surrender. That same day, a Royalist relief force led by the King and Prince Rupert, the King's nephew, arrived from Oxford and attacked Caversham Bridge. Fielding refused to break the truce by sending out troops from the town to help Prince Rupert, and the relief force was driven back. Terms for the Royalist surrender were agreed by Fielding on 26th April.

The following day, the Royalist soldiers marched away to Oxford and Essex's troops occupied Reading, which they plundered for two days before order was restored.

When he arrived at Oxford, Fielding was court-martialled for surrendering the town and sentenced to death. However, he was reprieved at the last minute because the king's teenage son, Charles, Prince of Wales, spoke up for Fielding, encouraged by Prince Rupert.

THE FORBURY AND THE ABBEY

14 Location: Information

panel, Chestnut Walk

Almost opposite the pillar
mentioned above is an
information panel which tells
you about Forbury Gardens
and the abbey ruins.

**Who established a Saxon
nunnery on the site, in
what year, and why?**

Who established the nunnery?

_____

In what year?

_____

Why?

_____

_____

15 Location: Commemorative plaque, Chestnut Walk

T.C.

Moving along the walk, with the river on your right, you come to a plaque placed on a short and low stone wall. It commemorates a poet and author who is associated with Reading. **Who was the poet, and why was the plaque placed here in the year 2000?**

Who was the poet?

Why was the plaque placed?

16 Location: 'Chocolate Island', Kennet bank

There is an island in the middle of the stream with a metal figure looking at the water. **What is he doing?**

_____

_____

17 Location: Toys R Us, Kennet bank

Continue walking along the river bank and you will see the back
wall of Toys R Us on your left. The names of towns are picked out
in brickwork on the building. **What towns are they, and why
do you think they are shown on this wall?**

What towns are they?

_____

_____

Why are they shown on the wall?

_____

_____

THE FORBURY AND THE ABBEY

18 Location: Gas Works Road Bridge

Carry on walking along the river bank and you will come to a green metal bridge across the river. Walk up the slope to the bridge, and at the start of the bridge you will see the Reading coat of arms with five faces, the central one wearing a crown. This is similar to the coat of arms on the pillars of the Palmer Park gates.

What company is mentioned, and what date?

What is the company?

_____

What is the date?

_____

19 Location: Information panel, Riverside Museum at Blake's Lock, Kenavon Drive

Walking further along the bank brings you to the Bel & The Dragon restaurant and the Riverside Museum at Blake's Lock. Look at the information panel close to the Museum.

a) **What are 'rymers'?**

_____

_____

b) **Can you work out what the purpose of a weir is?**

_____

_____

c) The Bel & The Dragon is situated in what was a pumping station. **What was the pumping station for?**

_____

_____

20 Location: Brunel railway bridge and Horseshoe Bridge.
Kennet bank at Kennet mouth, where the Kennet joins the
Thames in East Reading

On this old railway bridge is a small round plaque that
commemorates its architect, the great Isambard Kingdom Brunel.
The plaque also refers to the Horseshoe Bridge, which was built
later and attached to the railway bridge.

a) **What was the Horseshoe Bridge for?**

_____

_____

b) **When was it built?**

_____

c) **When was the railway bridge built?**

_____

Congratulations – you made it to the end! We hope you had fun on **The Forbury and the Abbey trail.** Turn to **page 136** to find out if you got all the answers right and to learn more about the town's links to Sherlock Holmes and the king who died from eating too many fish and was buried in Reading.

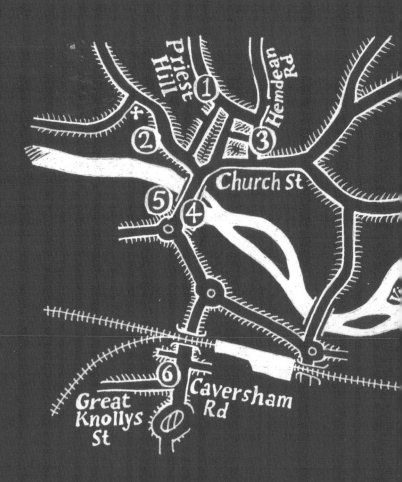

TRAIL 4: CAVERSHAM

CAVERSHAM

1   Location: Priest Hill, Caversham, RG4 7RZ

At the corner of Priest Hill and St Anne's Road is St Anne's Well.
An inscription tells you about the well.

**Who used to come to drink from the well in medieval
times? What qualities was the water thought to have?**

Who drank from the well?

_____

What were the qualities of the water?

_____

_____

2 Location: Caversham Court Gardens, Church Road

This is perhaps Reading's most beautiful public area, alongside the Thames on the north bank and close to Caversham Bridge.

There are several information panels in Caversham Court Gardens. Look at the panel located up the steps, in front of the churchyard.

2a) A famous Reading family lived at Caversham Court from 1799 – 1911. **Who were they, and why are they famous?**

Who are they?

_____

_____

Why are they famous?

_____

_____

2b) The wall separating the allotments from the churchyard is called a 'crinkle-crankle' wall. **What is unusual about it? Does 'crinkle-crankle' seem a good name?**

What is unusual?

_____

_____

Does 'crinkle-crankle' seem a good name?

_____

_____

2c) Find the little building called the Gazebo. On the path leading to its entrance there is a metal time-line. **Can you find the dates when the house was demolished and the gardens opened to the public?**

_____

3   Location: Hemdean Road, Caversham

There is an information panel at the bottom of Hemdean Road, near the corner of Church Road. The panel tells you about Caversham Library, which is situated on the same corner.

3a) **What creature is on the weather vane on the roof of the library?**

_____

3b) There is also a human figure supporting the clock
– who do you think he is?

_____

Did you know

Caversham
Bridge used to
be wooden till
halfway across
the river, and
then it turned
into stone.

The panel tells you about the Church
Street cottages, very ancient little houses
on Church Street, close to the start of
Caversham Bridge. They date from
the 1600s.

3c) **What are some of the
businesses that used to operate in
those cottages?**

_____

_____

_____

The panel also tells you about
Christchurch Meadows, off George Street,
Caversham.

3d) **Why are they called Christchurch
Meadows? When did Reading
Corporation take them over?**

_____

_____

_____

3e) By looking at the panel, **can you find a connection between Reading Town Hall, the Natural History Museum in London and two religious buildings in Caversham?**

_____

_____

Reading Bridge is referred to on the panel.

3f) **How did the builders test the strength of the bridge before it was opened in 1923, and what made it special at the time of its opening?**

_____

_____

Did you know ?

There was once a royal wedding in Reading.

Perhaps the most notable wedding that Reading ever saw was of John of Gaunt, fourth son of Edward III, and Blanche, his cousin, daughter of the Duke of Lancaster and a wealthy heiress. Poets such as Chaucer wrote about the beautiful couple, who became the parents of Henry IV.

They were married on 19 May 1359. He was 19, and said to be over seven feet in height. She was eighteen, beautiful with golden hair.

The marriage was performed by the Bishop of Salisbury, and among the guests were King Edward III and Edward the Black Prince.

Sadly, Blanche died of the plague only ten years after the wedding.

THE ABBEY

It is hard to appreciate today just how important Reading Abbey was for Reading and its development. For 400 years it completely dominated the little town, and the Abbot was the most important person in the region, collecting and spending taxes, and making and enforcing laws. Nothing could happen in Reading against the Abbot's will. However, as the centuries went by and the town grew, the townspeople found themselves in more and more disputes with the Abbot. The King sometimes had to intervene to settle these disputes. In the end the monarch asserted his power over the Church when Henry VIII closed all the monasteries and abbeys (the 'dissolution of the monasteries'). In Reading this involved the death of the Abbot as well as the closure and slow destruction of the once magnificent abbey. Hugh Faringdon, the Abbot, refused to agree to Henry's changes, and despite the two being old friends, the king ordered his execution in front of the Abbey Gateway on The Forbury – we can stand on that very spot today.

The abbey occupied a large space, about 30 acres, on what is now the Forbury Gardens, and covering Abbey Street and Abbey Square, the central library, St James

Church, and land alongside Chestnut Walk, next to the Prison. Forbury Road now follows a course skirting the east and north of the abbey grounds.

The abbey was founded by Henry I, the youngest son of William the Conqueror, in 1121. He gave the abbey his lands within Reading, and he also arranged for grants of further land in Reading and Sussex.

The original monks were from France. The abbey was built between the Rivers Kennet and the Thames and so had very good access, for travellers and trade. The River Kennet and the Holy Brook (a channel off the Kennet) provided power for the abbey watermills, and we can still see the arch of a mill just behind the Central Library. That mill went

Hugh Faringdon just prior to his hanging outside the abbey, 1539. He had been tied to a hurdle (a wooden frame) and dragged round the town to be jeered at by townspeople. The painting, by Harry Morley, is in Reading Museum.

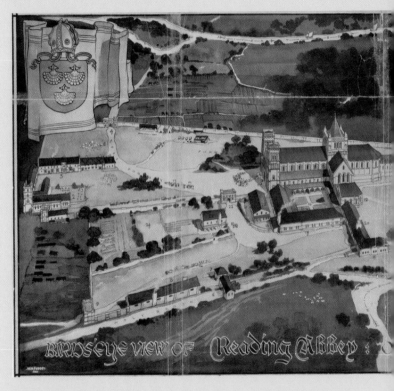

Aerial view of the abbey. St Laurence's Church is on the left. Towards the bottom is the mill, built over Holy Brook. The arch of the mill can still be seen, just behind the Central Library. The Forbury is the open space just to the left of the twin towers of the abbey, close to the Gateway, which still stands. Reading Gaol was built close to the long wall on the right.

on working well into the 20th century.

Henry I died before the abbey was completed and was buried there, in front of the altar. It is believed his body was later removed and it has disappeared.

The abbey was a pilgrimage centre of medieval England, and was one of the richest and most important religious houses, owning land as far away as Scotland. It held over 230 religious relics, including the hand of St James, which still survives in St Peter's RC Church, Marlow – though historians cannot be certain it is THE hand! Pilgrims would come from every part of the country, and from abroad, to worship at this very holy site, and also because they believed the relics had healing powers if they touched them, or bathed in water that had washed the relics. There were many stories of sick people who had been cured this way. The abbey would charge pilgrims for these visits and provide hospitality in the hospitium, which could accommodate several hundred people.

Reading Abbey was frequently visited by kings and important people, most frequently by Henry III, who often visited three or four times a year, staying several weeks on each visit. It also hosted important state events, such as the meeting between Henry II and the Patriarch of Jerusalem in 1185, the wedding of John of Gaunt in 1359 and the marriage announcement of Edward IV and

Elizabeth Woodville in 1464. There was a meeting of Parliament in the abbey in 1453.

After the Dissolution, much of the abbey was pulled down and the stone used for building, including repairs to the Minster Church at St Mary's Butts. The hospitium of the abbey, where guests and pilgrims stayed, was converted into a Town Hall, and a school. Over centuries, the abbey fell more and more into ruin, and care was taken to preserve the remains only from the 19th century on.

St James Catholic Church and School was built on abbey land and opened in 1840. It stands next to Reading Prison's main entrance. The Prison

The wedding of John of Gaunt and Blanche. On the throne is John's father, Edward III. The figure in dark robes, holding a scroll, is Geoffrey Chaucer. The painting, by Horace Wright, is in Reading Museum.

itself was built shortly after in 1844. The Forbury Gardens, in front of the still-existing Abbey Gateway, were opened by Reading Corporation in 1861.

What we see now are the inner rubble cores of the walls of some of the major abbey buildings, but only fragments of the Abbey Church still exist. The best preserved ruins are those of the chapter house, vestry, infirmary and dormitory. The site of the cloister is laid out as a private garden. The ruins are Grade I listed, meaning this is one of the most highly-valued historical sites in the UK. They are currently closed to visitors because of the danger of falling masonry, but a long-term restoration is under way under the direction of Reading Borough Council, who own the ruins. Eventually the area will open to the public again as one of the prime heritage sites of southern England.

The Importance of the Abbey

Food, clothing and money were given to the needy by the monks, and Reading was lucky in having the monastery as it provided the people with a kind of welfare system that other towns did not have. Education was also encouraged by the monks, who could read and write and would teach young men who might train to enter the monastery.

The abbey helped the growth of trade in the town. In Saxon times, before the abbey existed, the market was held in front of St Mary's Church, where St Mary's Butts is now. After 1121 it moved to near the abbey, in what is now Market Place. Much extra trade came from the visiting pilgrims staying in the hospitium nearby.

Major trading events were held three times a year, by special royal charter, inside the abbey walls in the large open area in front of the Abbey Church – the Forbury. These fairs each lasted for four days. They included entertainments but were mainly for the buying and selling of goods, people coming from miles around for the occasion. The noise was a great distraction to the monks in their silent daily routine.

Important visitors to the Abbot had to be accommodated, which caused a strain on the monks and the townspeople. A visit from the king included his family, their attendants and his guards and advisers and government officials. Hundreds of guests were involved. Lodgings would have to be found in the town as well as within the abbey, and a meeting of Parliament at the abbey would double the population of Reading.

Disputes Between the Abbot and the Townspeople

The abbey brought prosperity to the town, but there was still conflict between the town leaders and the Abbot, especially over choosing the mayor.

Over the years both sides took their case to the royal courts. It was eventually agreed that the Abbot could chose the Mayor from three candidates put to him by the merchants. Reading was unusual in continuing to argue with the Abbot and in achieving this compromise. Everywhere else in the country the Abbot won the upper hand.

The arguments between Abbot and ruling merchants took place in the Inner Gateway which we can still see on The Forbury. Here, in the long gallery over the archway, the two sides met. This Gateway continued in use after the abbey was dissolved. In the later 18th century it housed the Abbey School for Girls. It was restored in the 19th century and still stands.

One of the great figures in the restoration of the abbey was Dr Jamieson B. Hurry, who wrote a six-volume study of it, published at the start of the 20th century. He had the memorial to Henry I in the Forbury Gardens erected, and commissioned a number of history paintings about the abbey which are in the Reading Museum and Town Hall. His name is on the foundation stone for Battle Library in Oxford Road. He also wrote about medicine, social issues and botany, and died in 1930.

CAVERSHAM

4 Location: Caversham Bridge

The bridge links Caversham to Reading on the opposite bank of the Thames. Near the end of the bridge, on the right-hand side heading towards Reading, is an embossed metal plaque giving information about the bridge over its long history from 1231 to 1924.

4a) **What building once stood on the bridge? To whom was it dedicated?**

_____

_____

4b) **Which armies were in conflict on the bridge in 1643? Which Prince led one of the armies?**

_____

5   Location: Thames Side
     Promenade, just to the west
     of Caversham Bridge on the
     Reading side of the river

a) There is a drinking fountain here. **In whose memory was it built, what office did he hold, and when?**

_____

_____

b) Close by is an information panel. **What animals are not welcome on View Island?**

_____

c) **Where were the coalyards of the Great Western Railway?**

_____

CAVERSHAM

6 Location: Caversham Road, near the junction with Great Knollys Street

Dominic Barberi was a Catholic priest who died in a building on this spot.
What was the building?
In what year did he die?

What was the building?

_____

_____

What was the year?

_____

Now you've finished the **Caversham trail**, turn to **page 150** to see the answers. Were you right? Along with the answers, there's much more to learn about the special history of Reading, how it dates back to the Domesday Book and how the town's history is all around you every day.

1   Oxford Road. Battle Public Library
    Answer: **The foundation stone was laid by
    Dr Jamieson B. Hurry.**

Dr Jamieson Boyd Hurry also plays a major part in telling the
story of Reading Abbey, and in the setting up of the memorial to
Henry I. He was one of Reading's most notable people in the late
19th and early 20th centuries. His most important work was in
medical research, particularly concerning poor people.

Battle was the first branch library to be built by Reading Borough
Council. It was funded in part by Andrew Carnegie, a Scottish-born
multi-millionaire who made his fortune in America, and who gave
money for libraries all over the UK. It is a very special building and
has been a landmark for the local community since 1908. It is also
Grade II listed, so it is protected against development.

The first free public library in Reading came in 1875. William Isaac
Palmer, of the Huntley & Palmers biscuit firm, decided to pay for a
free library in West Street. This proved very popular, and managed
to win over people who thought that free libraries would be too
expensive to run.

From 1877 Reading Borough took responsibility for a library
service. The books of Reading Free Library were donated by
William Palmer to the Borough. A new museum and library
were added to the rebuilt Reading Town Hall, and this new
library opened in October 1882. For poor people, it was far too
expensive to buy books in those days, so a public library provided
a wonderful new opportunity, especially since most children were
then taught to read following the 1870 Education Act.

2   Oxford Road. The former Battle Hospital.
     Answer: **Private A. Challis died on 15th November, 1916.**

Very little is known about Private Challis.

Battle Hospital was originally a workhouse, opening in 1867.
Hospital accommodation for the poor was added, and in the First
World War it became 'No. 1 Reading War Hospital'. This war caused
far more British casualties than any other war, before or since.

During the First World War, activities were organised for the
military patients, and trips were arranged for them on the nearby
Thames. Nurses and doctors from the hospital were invited to
take part in the Victory Parade in Reading at the end of the war, to
honour their contribution to the war effort.

It was a general hospital, taking the name Battle Hospital, up until
2005 when it closed. One part of the grounds is now occupied by
a Tesco supermarket, and houses are being built on the other part.
The gatehouse on Oxford Road is almost all that remains. For many
Reading people, Battle Hospital is the place where they were born!

3   Oxford Road, corner of Russell Street. The Pavilion Church
     Answer: **It was Riley's snooker and pool club.**

You can see from the shape of the building that it used to be
a large cinema. The Pavilion Cinema opened in 1929, and it
became the Gaumont in 1958. It closed as a cinema in 1979,
became a bingo club, then Riley's snooker club. Some very
famous snooker players played exhibition matches there.

It is now a church, but with its original name from many years ago.

4   Goldsmid Road, behind Oxford Road

Answer: *It is the Reading Synagogue, where the Reading Hebrew or Jewish congregation worships.*

The onion dome is most famous as a feature of Russian churches, but there is disagreement as to the reason. It is probably from an eastern influence, such as the Mongol invasion of Russia in the 13th century. Some say the domes have the purpose of stopping snow from piling up on roofs. In Christian churches in Russia there are often three domes to represent the Holy Trinity. Muslim mosques and Jewish synagogues have also used the onion dome as a feature.

The Reading Hebrew congregation is said to date from 1886, and this synagogue, a grade II listed building, opened in 1900. However, there is evidence of a Jewish community in Reading from much earlier times.

5   55 Baker Street, off Russell Street, close to Castle Hill

Answer: *He was W.H. Fox Talbot, who lived there from 1844 to 1845. He is considered the father of modern photography.*

This house is a little-known but important historical site. William Henry Fox Talbot (1800–1877) was one of the pioneers of early photography, especially of the negative-positive method of making pictures. Born in Wales, he established a workshop in Baker Street, Reading. Here, in 1844, he manufactured the prints which made up the very first published book to be illustrated with photographs, The Pencil of Nature. The workshop no longer exists.

The house had previously been a school and most of the photographic work was carried out in a glasshouse adjoining the building, which Fox Talbot photographed. Many local people, including Mary Russell Mitford, were photographed here.

Reading Central Library has a collection of his early photographs of Reading dating from this time, and they can be seen online by typing 'Fox Talbot Illustrations' into the library catalogue search box. They are probably the earliest photographs of Reading in existence.

Fox Talbot was also an archaeologist and, for a short time, an MP.

6   Castle Street. The Almshouses

Answer: **They were built for six poor men**

Almshouses were built by charities, churches or by rich men who wanted to be remembered for good works after their death. They were designed as small and secure homes for old people who could no longer work and who had little money to support themselves. Many have been demolished around the country, but some remain. They are often interesting buildings and people like to live in them, especially if they have been modernised.

In Britain, almshouses date from the 10th century. The first recorded almshouse was founded in York by King Athelstan. The oldest still in existence is the Hospital of St Cross in Winchester, dating from about 1132.

In 1634 in Reading, almshouses were built in St Mary's Butts and were called 'St Mary's Almshouses'. They were the gift of Sir

Thomas Vachell after whom Vachell Street in central Reading is named. These old houses were demolished in 1867 and replaced with the buildings on Castle Street that we see today, with money coming from the sale of the St Mary's land. The new almshouses were renamed Vachel Almshouses. They were designed by the architect William Woodman, and were modernised in 1960–62.

The plaque at the entrance reads: 'Sr. Thomas Vachel Kt. erected there Alms-Houses Anno Dom. 1634, and endow'd them with Forty Pounds p. Annum for ever for the Maintenance of Six Poor Men.'

This refers to the original houses in St Mary's Butts. There are now 32 houses, all occupied, sought after and very well maintained.

7   **The Civic Centre. Spanish Civil War Memorial.**

Answer: **Mr Francis died at Aragon, in north-east Spain, in March 1938.**

Archibald Frank Francis was a 24-year-old insurance inspector from Reading. He threw up his job in Reading at short notice after he read about conditions in Madrid during the Spanish Civil War of 1936–39, and went over to Spain to fight against General Franco's Nationalist forces.

A civil war is a conflict within a country rather than between different countries. Men and women went from Britain and many other countries to help the democratic Republican side in Spain. They were afraid that if Franco's rebellion succeeded, it would encourage the dictators in Europe – Hitler and Mussolini – who supported Franco. Franco did succeed, and became dictator of Spain for nearly 40 years. (A dictator is someone who has total power – a tyrant). The Spanish Civil War was a preliminary to the Second World War and the great struggle of the democracies against the dictatorships of Germany, Italy and Japan.

8   **The Civic Centre. The cartwheeling boys sculpture, opposite the entrance.**

Answer: **It commemorates the link between Reading and Düsseldorf, in Germany. The boys are cartwheeling because it was traditional for boys in Düsseldorf to do this in exchange for a tip.**

Reading and Düsseldorf have had close ties since 1947, just after the end of the Second World War. The Mayor of Reading at that time, Phoebe Cusden, visited Düsseldorf to see conditions there, and saw a city devastated by Allied bombing. She organised help for the city and invited German children to stay in Reading. The first party of children, aged 12 to 14, arrived for an exchange visit in 1948, and were described as looking 'half-starved and ragged'.

Reading was the first British town after the Second World War to make a link with an 'enemy' city. The friendship has continued and grown ever since, and it is the oldest relationship of this kind between a British and a German city.

The sculpture is by Brian Slack, and it was unveiled in 1981.

9   **St Mary's Butts.**

Answer: **Queen Victoria's Golden Jubilee in 1887.**

St Mary's Butts is the main road in front of St Mary's Church. In the Middle Ages it was compulsory for all yeomen (farmers who owned land) in England to learn archery, so an archery butts, or target range, was set up on the land in front of the Minster Church. It was used by the men of Reading to practise archery on Sundays. Some of these men may have fought at the famous battle of Agincourt in 1415, when English archers defeated a much larger French army.

'Jubilee' is an old Hebrew word, now used to mean the celebration of an anniversary (25 years is a Silver Jubilee, 50 years is a Golden Jubilee and 60 years is a Diamond Jubilee). This memorial is for Queen Victoria's Golden Jubilee in 1887, when she had been queen for 50 years, and she went on to celebrate her Diamond Jubilee in 1897. In our times, Queen Elizabeth II celebrated her Diamond Jubilee in 2012, 60 years after her father, George VI, died.

10 **St Mary's Butts. St Mary's Church.**

Answer: **The merchant was Laurenthes Braag, who died in his 26th year, meaning he was 25 when he died.**

Laurenthes Braag was a young Danish merchant who died in Reading in 1808. At this time, Britain was at war with France and its allies which included Denmark. Danish merchants were detained in Reading because of the war but they had considerable freedom and were known as 'Gentleman Danes' because of their good behaviour. Braag and his friends were not the first Danes to visit Reading. Danish invaders had occupied the town and fought King Alfred nearby in 870 – nearly 1150 years ago!

St Mary's Church is possibly the most historic building in Reading. Its full title is Reading Minster of St Mary the Virgin.

When the Domesday Book was compiled in the 1080s, this Saxon Church was the only one in Reading. As a Minster Church, it was a kind of headquarters for the priests who were busy setting up smaller churches in the surrounding area. When it was rebuilt, it was with stones from the abbey, which slowly became a ruin after it was closed by Henry VIII.

William the Conqueror gave St Mary's Church and its land to Battle Abbey in Sussex, which is why we have 'Battle' names in Reading, such as the old Battle Hospital, Battle School, Battle Library and Battle Farm.

11 Bridge Street/Riverside, near The Oracle, opposite House of Fraser.

Answer a: **It took its water from artesian wells nearby.**

Answer b: **The Prince of Wales.**

The Prince of Wales (later Edward VIII) visited Reading on 25 June, 1926. The main event of the Prince's day was the opening of the new Caversham Bridge. The Berkshire Chronicle carried the headline: Where to See the Prince – the Complete Programme, and it was a very busy programme.

He also visited Suttons Seeds, the Co-op bakery, Simonds Brewery, the Royal Berkshire Hospital, Reading School, Huntley & Palmers, Huntley Boorne Stevens (who made biscuit tins), Reading University and finally a sports display at Palmer Park. Crowds turned out to see him throughout the town. The Prince's visits to areas suffering the economic depression of the 1920s and 1930s, on behalf of his father George V, made him very popular.

The information panel about the Simonds brewery is close to The Oracle shopping centre, one of the biggest in the south of England. But why is it called The Oracle? The name comes from the Oracle workhouse, built close to this site in the 17th century. The money for it was provided by a very famous figure from Reading's past – John Kendrick. He lived in the Tudor and Stuart periods of Elizabeth I and James I, having been born and educated in Reading. His school was located in the old abbey hospitium (place of accommodation for visitors and pilgrims), part of which is still there by St Laurence's Church.

Kendrick made a huge fortune as a cloth merchant in London, Reading and Newbury. When he died in 1624 he left money for the support of the poor, and workhouses were built in both the Berkshire towns. The Reading workhouse was called the Oracle, though there is dispute as to exactly why. It lasted over two hundred years and was demolished in 1850. When the shopping mall was opened in 1999, the historical name of the area was adopted.

Some of the Kendrick money was later used to found Kendrick Boys' School in 1875 and Kendrick Girls' School in 1877. The boys' school became the Reading School and Kendrick Girls' School remains. They are two of the outstanding grammar schools in England.

12 Oxford Road, corner of West Street.

Answer: **The store was McIlroy's.**

The McIlroy building was completed in 1903, and at the time was the largest department store outside London. It even had a hotel and staff accommodation at the top of the building, where you can see the smaller windows.

McIlroy's had so many plate glass windows it was known as the 'crystal palace'. It closed as a store in 1955. The ground floor was turned into individual shops. The upper floors have now been converted into fifty-eight apartments.

13 Broad Street. Waterstones bookshop.

Answer: **'Broad Street Independent Chapel' is engraved above the entrance. The galleries, where some of the congregation would sit, can clearly be seen inside the shop.**

Waterstones occupies what used to be the Broad Street Independent Chapel. It was a non-conformist chapel dating from the 1600s. Non-conformists were Protestant Christians who did not agree with the teachings of the Church of England, and who set up their own places of worship, such as the Methodist and Baptist churches and chapels.

The galleries of the main chapel now form part of the shop, with a sweeping staircase in the centre linking the two floors.

William Blackall Simonds, the founder of Simonds Brewery and J & C Simonds bank – both famous Reading businesses – was baptised at the chapel on 13 August 1761.

14 Broad Street. Moss menswear store.

Answer: **The animal is a bull, painted white. The lettering on the building shows that it used to be the Bull Hotel.**

Moss Brothers was a very famous company started by Moses Moss in Covent Garden in London in 1851. They won a great reputation as a supplier of tailoring at reasonable prices, and specialised in hiring out formal men's clothes for weddings and occasions such as Royal Ascot races. These were the sorts of clothes that only the rich could afford to own, so it was useful for people to hire them for a day or two quite cheaply. The company also did an important job supplying military uniforms in both World Wars. Today they have branches across Britain.

15 King Street. The George Hotel.

Answer: **Charles Dickens was the author.**

The George Inn was a coaching inn on the road between London and the West Country, for destinations such as Bath and Bristol. Before the building of the M4 in the 1960s, the main route to the west passed through the middle of Reading, via London Road and Bath Road. The town made a lot of money from this passing trade. By the late 1830s, ten different stage coaches passed through Reading every day. Different inns catered for different services. Ten years later there were no stagecoach services left, following the building of the railways.

Travellers would pass the night at The George, and fresh horses would be provided for the coach the next morning. Coaching inns always had plenty of stables. The 1700s would have been a busy time for The George, as Bristol and Bath were both very important at that time, and it was then that the inn would have got its name, from one of the several King Georges of the period.

Dickens changed coaches at The George on his way to the West Country, and may have stayed there on his occasional visits to Reading to give readings or performances.

16 King's Road. Girl and Swan sculpture

Answer: **Lorne McKean created the sculpture, which was unveiled on 28 June, 1984.**

Lorne McKean, born 1939, is a fellow of the Royal Society of British Sculptors. She is well known for her sculptures of animals in motion, including several birds in flight such as this. She has created sculptures of Prince Philip and Prince Andrew on horseback.

You can see a very interesting photograph of this sculpture while it was being created in the artist's studio at: www.lornemckean.com/The_Artist.html

17 King's Road. Huntley & Palmers building.

Answer: **The date shown is 1841. The parts of the plant are ears of wheat.**

1841 is when the partnership between Thomas Huntley and George Palmer was formed. They were distant cousins, and both members of the same religious group, the Quakers. The factory was actually started here in 1846 on the site of a silk mill, and later greatly expanded to fill 24 acres, (that's equivalent to about 15 football pitches!) with its own railway system and many tall chimneys.

In 1857, Thomas Huntley died, and his share was bought out by George Palmer and his brothers. But they kept the name of Huntley in the firm's title.

The ears of wheat on the company crest are to show the importance of flour as the biscuit factory's basic ingredient.

Both Huntley and Palmer are buried close to the Quaker Meeting House in Church Street, near the original shop on London Street.

TRAIL 2: NORTH TO EAST

1   Reading Station.

Answer: **He is King Edward VII, also Emperor of India. The statue was donated by Martin John Sutton, head of the Suttons Seeds firm from 1887.**

Edward VII was king from 1901 to 1910. Because his mother reigned for so long, over 63 years, Edward was quite elderly (59) when he eventually became king. His period as monarch is known as the Edwardian era. On the back of the statue you can see some of the celebrations listed from his Coronation in 1902.

It was Edward's mother, Queen Victoria, who took the title of Empress of India in 1877, at the suggestion of the Prime Minister, Benjamin Disraeli. It was hoped that the title would make the Indians feel more loyal towards the monarchy. Victoria's successors took the same title until India became independent in 1947. On old British coins you will see the words 'Ind. Imp.', short for 'Indiae Imperator', the Latin for Emperor of India.

As Prince of Wales and the heir to the throne, Edward came to Reading in 1870 to lay the foundation stone of the present Reading School.

2   Station Road. Malmaison Hotel.

Answer: **The Great Western Railway was the name of the company that built the line from London to Reading, completed in 1840. The Malmaison used to be called the Great Western Hotel until the 1960s.**

Isambard Kingdom Brunel was once thought to have designed this hotel building, though historians now say that's unlikely. He was the Great Western Railway's chief engineer when the hotel was built. It is one of the oldest surviving railway hotels in Britain, dating from 1844, four years after Reading Station opened in 1840. Railway companies often built luxurious hotels near their important stations, and Reading was a key station on the Great Western Railway, which Brunel built westwards from Paddington towards Bristol.

After 1840, Reading to London took only 65 minutes by rail, a quarter of the time of the quickest stage coach. So the opening of the station made day trips to London's museums, theatres and shops possible for the first time. The Duke of Wellington would come to Reading from his house in the country and load his carriage onto the train for London, so he could use it at the other end!

3   Friar Street. Yates's pub, formerly the Post Office.

   Answer: **The building used to be the Post Office. The words 'Post Office' can still be seen above the entrance.**

The 'General Post Office' in London was founded by Charles II in 1660. For centuries it was under the monarch's control, and today our postal service is still called the 'Royal Mail'.

The first local post office in Britain was in Scotland, and dates from 1712. After the national 'Penny Post' was introduced in 1840, and railways could carry mail quickly all over the country, all towns and many villages would have a post office. Britain was the first country in the world to have postage stamps.

This building, which is on the site of the old Queen's Hotel, was converted to a pub in the 1990s. The Post Office moved a few yards down the road, close to the Town Hall, where it is today.

Yates's is Britain's oldest pub chain. There are still over 70 Yates's in the UK, though there used to be many more. The first Yates's Wine Lodge opened in Oldham in 1884.

Many banks and post offices have closed over the past two decades, and it was common for the buildings to be taken over by pubs.

4   Friar Street/Blagrave Street. Queen Victoria's statue, outside the Town Hall.

Answer: **Arthur Hill was the Mayor of Reading on four occasions. Queen Victoria is missing one of her fingers.**

The statue of Victoria is another creation of the sculptor George Blackall Simonds, who also sculpted the Maiwand Lion in the Forbury Gardens. When bombs fell close to the statue in 1943, the tip of one of the Queen's fingers was blown off, and it is now in Reading Museum.

Arthur Hill was the half-brother of Octavia Hill, one of the founders of the National Trust. The swimming baths near Cemetery Junction, which opened in 1911, commemorate his name. He also bought the copy of the world-famous Bayeux Tapestry for Reading Museum in 1895. It had been created by the ladies of the Leek Embroidery Society in Staffordshire and had been on show in Reading Town Hall. It is still one of the Museum's great attractions.

(Find out more at www.readingmuseum.org.uk)

5   Blagrave Street. Reading Town Hall.

Answer: **The date above the Town Hall entrance is 1875.**

The Town Hall was built in several stages between 1786 and 1897. The main frontage we see today was designed by the famous architect Alfred Waterhouse (who also designed the Natural History Museum in London) and it was erected in 1875. His 'Gothic Revival' style was inspired by the great cathedrals of the Middle Ages. He lived in Reading from the late 1860s, and also designed Foxhill House on Reading University Campus, St Bartholomew's Church and Reading School.

The Town Hall stands close to the site of the old Reading Abbey. St Laurence's Church, built by the monks of the abbey, is close by.

It was in the Town Hall that all the important business of the town was carried out, and where councillors met. Today that happens in the Civic Centre, and the Town Hall houses the Museum, a cafe, a concert hall and rooms for weddings and celebrations.

6   Blagrave Street. Town Hall, first floor, display case.

Answer: **The plaque marks the death of Margaret Thackeray, who worked at the Town Hall, in the German bombing raid of Wednesday 10 February, 1943.**

More than 40 people were killed, and about 150 injured – many of them in the People's Pantry restaurant just opposite the Town Hall. Margaret Thackeray was on duty in the Town Hall at the time. In those days shops in Reading closed on Wednesday afternoons otherwise many more people may have been killed and injured. The author of the Paddington Bear stories – Michael Bond – then aged 17, was in the People's Pantry at the time but was fortunate enough to survive.

Bombs also fell in Minster Street and Wellsteed's Department store was destroyed. In all, four bombs fell on the town centre. This was by far the worst bombing raid on Reading, which was not a target town. For security reasons the newspapers couldn't name Reading and referred in their stories to a raid on 'a Home Counties town'. The German bomber was shot down later that day in Sussex.

In 2013 a plaque was unveiled on the wall of Blandy and Blandy Solicitors, between the Town Hall and St Laurence's Church, to commemorate the 70th anniversary of the tragedy.

7   Blagrave Street. Town Hall, first floor.

Answer: **Edward IV is announcing that he is married to Elizabeth Woodville in Reading Abbey in 1464.**

This was a spectacular and colourful event involving a Council of Peers, or Lords. It was painted by Ernest Board in 1923.

King Edward IV was a major figure in the Wars of the Roses between the Royal Houses of York (the White Rose) and Lancaster (the Red Rose) who contested the right to the crown. Edward was a Yorkist. Elizabeth Woodville was the mother of 'the Princes in the Tower', who were supposedly murdered on the orders of Edward's brother, Richard Duke of York (later Richard III).

Elizabeth was a powerful figure in her own right during the Wars of the Roses, and she was the first 'commoner' to marry an English monarch since 1066. She was the grandmother of Henry VIII, and is 'The White Queen' in the book by Philippa Gregory.

Although this painting seems to show a wedding, it was actually the occasion when Edward declared Elizabeth to be his wife. They had already been married privately on May Day. The marriage ceremony was kept secret because she was not of royal blood, her family was not popular and the couple knew there would be opposition to their marriage.

8   Market Place and Friar Street. St Laurence's Church.

Answer: **The fountain was built in 1860 – very recently, compared to the church. The sundial is dated 1727.**

St Laurence's Church stands very close to where the abbey once stood. The church itself dates from the Norman period (12th century) and the tower from 1458.

The private chapel of the abbey's hospitium (a dormitory for travellers or pilgrims) was located in the north aisle of the church.

St Laurence's was one of the three original parish churches, along with St Mary's and St Giles', in the medieval borough of Reading. It was built for the people of the eastern part of the town. Its location next to the abbey encouraged trade in that part of the town.

St Laurence's soon became surrounded by a large marketplace, which included a pillory and stocks for punishing wrong-doers. The Market Place, of course, is still there.

Elizabeth I often stayed in Reading and attended services at this church, where she had a special seat. She would visit the house of her Principal Secretary, Sir Francis Walsingham, who lived on the corner of Broad Street and Minster Street, where number 134 is today.

The sundial is dated 1727 and has the inscription 'Vigilate et Orate', Latin for 'Watch and Pray'. Traders in the marketplace would have found it useful to glance up at the Tower to read the time.

9   St Laurence's Churchyard.

Answer: **Henry West, a workman aged 24, was working on the roof of the new Reading Station just before it opened in 1840. A high wind, described as a 'whirlwind', blew him off the roof and a distance of 200 feet to his death.**

The original memorial, in the form of a rail, was placed by his workmates. The current one dates from the 1970s. There is also a memorial plaque to Henry on Reading Station.

10 St Laurence's Churchyard and the hospitium.
    The dancing figures.

Answer: **The sculptor was Liz Mulchinock and the date of the sculpture is 1983.**

The statue, called 'Adam, Libby and Karen', is located just outside the renovated hospitium of Reading Abbey, now used as a day nursery. A hospitium was a dormitory and guest house for travellers and pilgrims to the abbey. At one time the abbey could accommodate 400 guests. It offered two free days of board and lodging to pilgrims.

After the dissolution of the abbey in 1539, the hospitium continued to be used as the Abbey School and as Reading's Town Hall before the present Town Hall began to be built in the late 1700s. It was also the first home for the college which later became Reading University.

11 Market Place. The Simeon 'Monument'.

Answer: **Edward Simeon paid for the structure.**

Edward Simeon was a director of the Bank of England. He commissioned this structure in 1804, and it was designed by Sir John Soane. It carried lamps to improve the lighting of Market Place. Some said it was to win votes for his older brother, John Simeon, who was standing for Parliament for Reading! Towns at that time were badly lit and dangerous with many robberies, especially at night. This is often referred to as the Simeon Monument, but it is not really a monument – more of an elaborate lamp post!

Sir John Soane was a very famous architect of the time, born in Goring or Whitchurch, near Reading, and attending school in Reading. He designed a brewery and a house for the Simonds brewing family on Bridge Street, demolished in 1900. His house in London is now a wonderful free museum, full of his treasures.

The museum is at 13 Lincoln's Inn Fields, London WC2A 3BP. www.soane.org

12 Market Place. Market Way.

Answer: **The building was originally the Corn Exchange.**

A corn exchange was a market where farmers, dealers, shop-keepers, etc., would buy and sell cereals such as wheat and barley, sheltered from the weather. Reading was the main market town for Berkshire agriculture. There were hundreds of corn exchanges all over Britain in the 19th and early 20th centuries, but now the trade is done in a few large centralised locations, rather than locally. The Corn Exchange buildings came to be used for other purposes, such as a shopping arcade in Reading and a theatre in Newbury. The tower is all that remains of the original Corn Exchange, as most of it was destroyed in the bombing of 10 February, 1943.

13 Duke Street Bridge, or High Bridge.

Answer: **The bridge was rebuilt in 1788.**

This bridge, also known as High Bridge, was the main route into town from London and the south. Thousands of carters' wagons would have crossed the Kennet here over the centuries. Alongside the bridge you will see the pathway called Highbridge Wharf, which is a reminder that many goods were carried through Reading on the canal and the river, and loaded and unloaded in the town.

14 Mill Lane.

Answer: **The engraved plaque refers to the electric tram.**

The Imperial Tramways Company used to provide horse-drawn tram routes in Reading in the late 1800s. It was bought in 1901 by the Reading Corporation who decided to electrify the system. Reading Corporation Electric Tramways moved to this site, the Mill Lane depot, in 1903 when the first electric tram car service began. The new Tramways Depot site had previously been a brass foundry, the old Reading water works and St Giles' Mill, which is why it was called Mill Lane.

The new depot included the Tramways Power Station. When the electric trams were introduced there was no national power supply, so a boiler house and generating station were built at the new tramways depot.

The first electric trams caused great excitement in the town, and huge crowds turned out for the opening journeys. They were the height of modern urban transport. The main route was from Wokingham Road, through the town centre and out along Oxford Road, similar to today's 17 bus route. Trams on this route would run every 5 minutes. There were also routes along Caversham Road and down to Whitley, and along Bath Road and Erleigh Road.

Motor buses were introduced in 1919, and eventually proved much more flexible than trams. Trolley buses replaced trams from 1936 on, and trams ceased to run in 1939. The trolley buses, in turn, were phased out in 1968, and replaced by buses. The Mill Lane depot was used for all three means of transport. It was demolished in 1998 to make way for The Oracle.

There are a number of excellent photos of Reading trams to be seen on the internet.

15 London Street. The Great Expectations pub.

Answer: **Sampson Brass is the character.**

Charles Dickens gave readings of his works in this building on two occasions, and it housed the Literary and Mechanics' Institute, of which he was President. It was at various times a theatre, a chapel and a warehouse, and became a pub in the 1990s. It is called 'Great Expectations' after one of Dickens' most famous novels. He also acted in a play he had written, in a special performance for charity, in Reading Town Hall in 1851. The cast included some of his well-known friends such as Wilkie Collins and Sir John Tenniel. When Dickens came to Reading he may have stayed in The George Hotel.

These cartoons are of characters and scenes from his novels. Sampson Brass was in The Old Curiosity Shop and was a cheating

TRAIL 2: NORTH TO EAST

lawyer who pretended to have feelings for his clients.

Dickens was asked to stand as MP for Reading but he turned down the offer. There is another Reading connection with Dickens: Sir Thomas Noon Talfourd was an MP for Reading, and a friend of Dickens. He put through a bill in Parliament to protect authors' copyright, to stop their works being stolen by others. Dickens was so grateful that he dedicated The Pickwick Papers to his friend Talfourd, and he attended his funeral in 1854. The MP is himself commemorated in the name of Talfourd Avenue, in East Reading.

16 London Street. Addington House, on the left hand side going up the hill.

Answer: **Anthony Addington was the physician, or doctor, to King George III, and his son Henry Addington became Prime Minister in 1801.**

Addington House was Dr Addington's home, and the building next door was his surgery, where patients sometimes stayed. The doctor was born in Twyford in 1713, and he was a doctor in Reading until 1754, when he left for London. He practised medicine there for twenty years and became well known. He treated such famous men as Pitt the Elder and Pitt the Younger, both of whom were important Prime Ministers. Addington's son, Henry, became Prime Minister in 1801, and it was he who donated the land on which the Royal Berkshire Hospital was built. Addington Road, near the Hospital, is named after him. He later became Lord Sidmouth and gave his name to Sidmouth Street, near Kendrick School.

London Street used to be a fashionable shopping street, and was the scene of great festivity in 1814. To celebrate victory over Napoleon, a public dinner was provided for 6,000 poor people, and the tables stretched from the top of London Street through to Friar Street. Six thousand people was about half the population of the town back then!

17 **121 London Street. Huntley House.**

Answer: **The plaque marks the founding of the first Huntley shop on this site in 1826, which grew into Huntley & Palmers, the biggest biscuit company in the world.**

See 'The Three B's' on page 8 to find out more.

18 **London Road. Kendrick View House.**

Answer: **The author was Mary Russell Mitford, writer of 'Our Village'.**

Mary Russell Mitford lived in the house as a girl. Her father bought the house with money that ten-year-old Mary had won in a lottery – £20,000 – which would be equivalent to millions of pounds today. Unfortunately her father was a spendthrift and a gambler and eventually lost all the prize money. For many years they lived in a humble farm cottage at Three Mile Cross, near Reading. Mary based her successful stories in 'Our Village' on Three Mile Cross.

She also wrote a novel based on life in Reading, called 'Belford Regis'.

19 London Road. The Royal Berkshire Hospital.

Answer: **The first three surgeons were G. May, T.B. Maurice, and F.A. Bulley. They all began work in 1839.**

The 'Royal Berks' was opened in 1839 on land donated by Henry Addington, a local resident and former Prime Minister (see Answer 16 for more information about Henry Addington). It is built in a classical style with imposing columns at the London Road entrance. The architect was Henry Briant, whose design won a competition. The entrance has a large triangular pediment supported by six Ionic columns in the style of ancient Greece. The building is built from Bath stone, brought from the West Country to Reading on the Kennet and Avon canal, as this was before the railway existed. King William IV took a great interest in the building – his coat of arms appears above the entrance and the hospital was allowed to call itself 'Royal'. William died before the hospital opened, but his niece and successor, Queen Victoria, became its first patron.

The East and West wings were added in the 1860s. The Hospital laundry, built in 1881, is now a medical museum.

The Duchess of Cambridge and her sister Pippa were born at the Royal Berks., and the pilot Douglas Bader had both legs amputated there, but still went on to become a famous flying 'ace' during the Second World War.

The hospital is one of the biggest employers in the town, with about 4,000 staff.

20 Eldon Square, King George V Memorial Gardens. Statue of
     Rufus Isaacs, Marquess of Reading.

Answer: **He is holding a book.**

This statue was originally located in Coronation Park in Delhi,
India, in 1935. It was moved to this spot in 1971.

From humble beginnings in East London, Rufus Isaacs became a
barrister and an MP. In the governments of the early 1900s, he was
Attorney General, Foreign Secretary, Lord Chief Justice, Ambassador
to the USA and Viceroy of India. He was knighted and later became
Marquess of Reading. This is the highest rank in the peerage
reached by a Jew in British history. He was also the first Jew who
practised his religion to be appointed to the British Cabinet.

For some time Rufus Isaacs lived at Foxhill House, which is now
home to the Law Faculty of Reading University in Whiteknights
Park. He was MP for Reading from 1904 to 1913. His name is not
engraved on the statue, but there is a Latin inscription which
seems to have been wrongly spelled, but which means 'If you are
going to do something, do it perfectly'. He died in 1935.

Eldon Square was Reading's first conservation area, because
of the surrounding houses which are built of beautiful Bath
stone, like the Hospital. It is named after Lord Eldon, who was
Lord Chancellor in the government of Lord Addington in the
early 1800s. Eldon was a supporter of the founding of the Royal
Berkshire Hospital.

21 Cemetery Junction, Old Reading Cemetery.

Answer: **Motorcycle and aeroplane were the two forms of travel. Bernard died aged 21.**

Bernard Laurence Hieatt was an air pilot and motorcycle racer. He came from Reading, where his father ran a butcher's business. He died in an accident at the Brooklands race track in Surrey on May 3rd, 1930, having flown himself to the meeting from Woodley Aerodrome. He was the holder of two world records in motorcycle/sidecar racing, and he broke two records at Brooklands on the day he died.

During the funeral service aeroplanes encircled the church, and one, which belonged to the late pilot, flew black streamers from wings and tail. Planes followed the coffin along the Wokingham Road and after the burial, dipped wings to give the airman's salute. As they flew low over the cemetery, they dropped a laurel wreath attached to a parachute.

22 War Memorial, Old Reading Cemetery.

Answer: **Two countries from Australia, New Zealand and Canada.**

As with nearly all British cemeteries, there is a war memorial for the two World Wars of the 20th century. There are hundreds of servicemen buried here, partly because Reading had several hospitals for soldiers during the First World War, such as Battle Hospital and the temporary hospital at Wilson Road School.

The cemetery was built in 1842 on farmland just outside the old borough boundary, which ran between Eastern Avenue and Carnarvon Road. The owner of the land was Mr Cholmeley, after whom a road is named in Newtown. Victorian towns were growing so fast that finding burial sites was a problem, and Reading's parish church graveyards were filling up.

This cemetery was one of the new style 'garden' cemeteries. The cemetery used to be divided into two parts by a wall – one part for Church of England members, the other for non-conformist believers, such as Presbyterians or Baptists.

Other notable memorials are for George Blackall Simonds, sculptor of the Maiwand Lion in Forbury Gardens; Joseph Edward Sydenham, the founder of Reading Football Club who died in 1913; and William 'Willie' Wimmera, an Aboriginal Australian boy who died in 1852 from tuberculosis, aged 11, after missionaries had brought him to Reading.

23 **Palmer Park Gates, Wokingham Road.**

Answer: **They are sea shells – actually scallop shells.**

The shells were symbols of the pilgrims who often visited Reading Abbey, and shells have formed part of the Borough of Reading's coat of arms at various times. The origin of the story is that shells are the traditional symbol for Saint James, and scallop shells were carried by pilgrims to the shrine of Santiago de Compostela in Northern Spain. Santiago is Spanish for Saint James.

The relic of the hand of St James was given to Reading Abbey by Maud, daughter of Henry I, and it became one of the chief objects of pilgrimage to the abbey. So the shells are a symbol both of St James and of pilgrims, both of which are relevant to Reading. There is now a St James Church very close to the abbey ruins, next door to Reading Prison.

TRAIL 2: NORTH TO EAST

There is an excellent double meaning in the scallop shells outside Palmer Park, as 'palmer' is an ancient word for 'pilgrim'. A 'palmer' was a pilgrim who had brought a palm leaf back from the Holy Land. They represent the pilgrims, or palmers, who were so important to medieval Reading, and they remind us of George Palmer.

The five faces on the centre carving may be Saxon figures. The central one wearing the crown is possibly Edward, King of the English (975–78), who was murdered at the orders of his step-mother Elfrida. It was she who had the nunnery at St Mary's Butts first built as a sign of repentance for her sin. In other versions of these figures, which appear on the official seal of Reading, the figures are maidens with long hair.

The town coat of arms on the bridge in Gasworks Road has the same figures and the letters 'RE', which may stand for 'Regina Elizabeth', Latin for 'Elizabeth the Queen'. Elizabeth I was Queen when the arms were first granted by the monarch in 1566. The five faces, whoever they may be, are first seen on the town seal in the 14th century.

24 **Wokingham Road, Palmer Park. The George Palmer statue.**

Answer a: **He was Reading's MP from 1878 to 1885.**

Answer b: **He was Mayor of Reading from 1857 to 1858.**

The statue was unveiled in the middle of Broad Street in 1891, the same day that Palmer Park opened. In 1930 it was moved from Broad Street to its current home in Palmer Park, as it was causing traffic problems in the centre of town. The land for the park was given to the town in 1889 by the Palmer family, of the Huntley &

Palmers biscuit company, which is why the statue of George Palmer was put here.

George Blackall Simonds was the sculptor – he was also the creator of the Maiwand Lion in the Forbury Gardens. He was criticised for showing Palmer holding an umbrella, with rather creased trousers! He was a director of the Simonds brewing company, a famous Reading family firm that provided many jobs. They were responsible for the 'beer' in Reading's 'Three B's'.

See 'The Three B's' on page 8 to find out more.

TRAIL 3: THE FORBURY AND THE ABBEY

1 The Forbury. Forbury Gardens. The War Memorial.

Answer: **The Memorial is dedicated: 'To the honoured memory of the men of Reading and Berkshire who gave their lives for King and Country during the Great Wars'.**

Like other such monasteries, Reading Abbey had a forbury, an area of open land in front of the abbey which provided a meeting place between the abbey and the town. The forbury in Reading provided a marketplace as well as a meeting place. Most of the area is now a park in the centre of Reading, called the Forbury Gardens.

The Royal Berkshire Regiment was awarded 55 battle honours, and two of its members gained Victoria Crosses during World War I, 1914–18. The Regiment suffered 7,140 casualties during that war.

The designer of the memorial was Leslie Gunston, who was a cousin of the war poet Wilfred Owen. It was not erected until 1932, because of the difficulty in raising funds for it. An earlier attempt straight after the war to put up a 'Winged Victory' memorial had failed for lack of money.

2 The Forbury. Forbury Gardens. Information panel at main entrance to Forbury Gardens.

Answer: **Suttons Seeds helped with the Gardens.**

See 'The Three B's' on page 8 to find out more.

3   The Forbury. Forbury Gardens. The Maiwand Lion.

Answer: **There are six Private Smiths. The places in Afghanistan are Girishk and Kandahar.**

The Forbury Lion is also known as the Maiwand Lion, named after the 1880 Battle of Maiwand, in Afghanistan. It was erected in 1886 to commemorate the deaths of 329 men from the 66th (Berkshire) Regiment of Foot during the campaign in Afghanistan between 1878 and 1880. Sir Arthur Conan Doyle based his character Doctor Watson, Sherlock Holmes' friend, on the regiment's Medical Officer, Surgeon Major A. F. Preston, who was injured in battle.

The sculptor of the lion was George Blackall Simonds, a member of the Reading brewing family, who also sculpted Queen Victoria's statue outside the Town Hall.

4   The Forbury. Forbury Gardens. The *Ilex* tree.

Answer: **The tree was planted in honour of the marriage of the Duke of York to Princess Mary Victoria of Teck on 6th July 1893.**

'Ilex' is the Latin name for the holly family, so this is a type of holly tree.

The Duke of York went on to become King George V, grandfather of Elizabeth II. He died in 1936, and was succeeded by his son Edward VIII, who gave up the throne before he could be crowned. He wanted to marry a divorced woman, and the Church of England and the Prime Minister disapproved of this. Edward was succeeded by his brother George VI, father of Elizabeth II.

TRAIL 3: THE FORBURY AND THE ABBEY

5   The Forbury. Forbury Gardens. Forbury Hill

Answer: **Joshua Vines, a well-known landscape gardener of the Victorian period, was the director.**

This small hillock of raised ground in the Forbury is all that remains of the fortifications from the English Civil War in the 1640s.

The Civil War was fought between the forces of King Charles I (the Royalists or Cavaliers) and the forces of Parliament (the Roundheads), led by Oliver Cromwell. The Roundheads eventually won, and Charles I was executed in 1649.

Reading played an important role during that War. It had a Royalist army base, and the town's tailors were forced to make a thousand suits of cloth for the king's soldiers. The Royalists squeezed a lot of money out of the townspeople. Reading was besieged by Parliamentary forces, who overcame the Royalists in April 1643 in a struggle at Caversham Bridge. The town's cloth trade was especially badly damaged, and Reading's prosperity did not fully recover for many years.

See 'The Bridges.' on page 68 to find out more.

6   The Forbury. Forbury Gardens. King Henry's memorial.

Answer: **Dr Jamieson B. Hurry erected the monument on 18 June, 1909.**

Henry I founded Reading Abbey in 1121 and was buried there. This memorial stands where the west door of the Abbey Church once was.

King Henry chose to make the abbey his family burial place. He died in France in 1135, before the building work was complete.

The Royal body was embalmed, wrapped in bulls' hides and shipped back to Reading for burial in front of the abbey's High Altar. His funeral was attended by Queen Adeliza, (Henry's second wife), the new King, Stephen, and most of the leading churchmen and nobles of England. A hundred shillings was granted for the maintenance of a lamp to burn constantly over his grave, and an image of the monarch was later placed over the grave.

Some believed that King Henry was buried in a silver coffin and perhaps this is why workmen much later broke into his tomb. Finding only a stone coffin, they scattered the Royal bones.

Today King Henry is remembered by this large memorial cross in the Forbury Gardens and a small plaque in the South Transept of the ruined abbey, close to his last resting place.

7   **The Forbury. The Forbury Hotel, facing Forbury Gardens.**

Answer: **Berkshire County Council occupied the building, in 1911 – which is actually at the very beginning of George V's reign.**

This luxury hotel was originally built in 1911 as a headquarters for Berkshire County Council and was known then as the Shire Hall. Full council meetings were in the Assize Court building next door. In 1980 the council moved to a new Shire Hall in Shinfield Park and afterwards this building in The Forbury was converted into offices.

In 2006, it was turned into a luxury hotel. It has a beautiful chandelier inside with 86,000 glass beads, and it also has a small cinema for guests.

8   The Forbury. The Crown Court building.

Answer: **A harp, the symbol of Ireland, is the musical instrument. It is the British monarch's coat of arms.**

In the Royal coat of arms, the shield is supported by a lion and a unicorn. On the shield, the three lions of England are represented twice. We see the same three lions on the England football shirt. The lion of Scotland is also shown, as well as the harp representing Ireland. There seems to be nothing for Wales! This is because there is a separate coat of arms for the Prince of Wales.

This building in Reading was built as an Assize Court in 1861, and judges would travel to the town to hear cases, though by that time they would travel on the Great Western Railway! Henry II set up Assize Courts in 1166, and they lasted until 1972, when Crown Courts replaced them.

Assize Courts had judges who would travel around the country, trying cases and appointing juries on behalf of the king or queen. The High Sheriff and other important citizens would ride out to the edge of town to greet the judge in a colourful ceremony. He would often be accompanied by barristers and their families, and they would be taken to their lodgings with church bells pealing.

9   The Forbury. The Abbey Gateway.

Answer: **The gateway was restored by Sir George Gilbert Scott. It had collapsed during a great storm.**

It was originally the inner gateway of Reading Abbey, leading from the public open space of the Forbury into the monks' private area. The Blessed Hugh Faringdon, last Abbot of the abbey, was hanged outside the gateway in 1539, having been tried in his own courtroom in the room above the gateway's arch.

It was used by Reading Ladies' Boarding School in the late 1700s and the famous author Jane Austen and her sister Cassandra went to school there in 1785–86.

The gateway partially collapsed in 1861, having been poorly maintained by the Reading Corporation, and was rebuilt by the noted architect Sir George Gilbert Scott in a kind of 'Victorian medieval' style. Scott reused the medieval features from the 12th to 14th centuries. It is a Grade I listed building, so is protected in law. Sculpted on to the side of the gateway are scallop shells, the symbol of the pilgrims visiting the abbey.

The Abbey Gateway has been used in recent years for community activities such as film clubs and art groups, and for small church services.

Scott was one of the most famous of Victorian architects and was responsible for the Albert Memorial and St Pancras Station Hotel in London, and many other notable buildings including Reading Prison.

10 Abbots' Walk, continuation of The Forbury, alongside the Gardens. Information plate at end of Abbot's Walk, in front of fence, and abbey ruins.

Answer a: **'The Burial of Henry I' was painted by Harry Morley in 1916.**

Answer b: **A bell and belfry are on the roof of the school building, which is now used as a nursery. The bell would be rung to tell the children that school was about to start and that they must not be late.**

There is a legend that Henry I died through eating too many lampreys, a kind of small fish which resemble eels.

He had three legitimate children, and supposedly more than twenty illegitimate children! No legitimate male heir survived him, which caused huge difficulty after his death. It was thought of as a great problem to have a woman on the throne. Henry wanted his daughter, Matilda, to reign after him, but she was opposed by Henry's nephew, Stephen, who succeeded in becoming King Stephen.

During the Second World War, this school – the church school of St James next door – made use of air raid shelters that had been dug underneath Forbury Gardens. The school is built just about where the abbey's nave and altar were, many hundreds of years before. See 'The Abbey' on page 94 to find out more.

11 Abbey Street. Abbey Gardens. The Frink Sculpture.

Answer: **Elisabeth Frink created the sculpture in 1988.**

Elisabeth Frink, who died in 1993, was a very famous British sculptor. She concentrated on figures of very masculine men, occasionally women, and animals (especially horses). Her sculptures often show strong figures moving across ground. She was one of a number of British Women of Achievement commemorated on postage stamps by the Royal Mail in 1996.

12 Abbey Street. Abbey Gardens. The sculpture.

Answer: **The sculptor was Jens-Flemming Sørensen, 2000.**

The sculpture, or installation, is entitled 'Ball Heads'. Sørensen (born in 1933 in Denmark) is a sculptor of figures. His work is featured in many public spaces, but this appears to be his only public sculpture in the UK. Sørensen often finds inspiration in forms of nature when making his sculptures. He likes to form human body parts, or spheres or obelisks, which seem to be breaking out of the stone they are encased in.

This is an especially good location to see the abbey ruins. Here we can view the remaining walls of the refectory (dining hall), the dormitory (sleeping room) and the chapter house. In the chapter house the monks would listen to readings from scriptures and discuss abbey business.

13 Chestnut Walk

Answer: **The wharf was for unloading goods and supplies for the abbey.**

The wharf is on the Kennet, near where it meets the Thames. All sorts of building materials and farm produce would be carried by river, which was much more reliable than the roads. Wheat in particular was carried across South East England on the Thames, Kennet and other rivers. The Romans built excellent roads, but after they left Britain in about 400 AD, the roads fell into disrepair, and were not really rebuilt properly until the late 18th century and after.

The abbey bought a lot of goods for the monks, for other people who lived there, and for pilgrims and guests. The abbey would also grow a lot of its own food, and possibly have fish ponds. The area around the abbey, including the Forbury, was used as a market-place where the townspeople would buy and sell goods that would be moved by river.

TRAIL 3: THE FORBURY AND THE ABBEY

14 Chestnut Walk.

Answer: **Queen Elfrida established the nunnery in 979, in penance for the murder of her stepson, King Edward.**

The nunnery was built where St Mary's Butts now is, and it was the first Christian establishment in Reading. It was destroyed by the Danes in their invasion of 1006, when Elfrida's son, Ethelred the Unready, was King of England.

15 Chestnut Walk

Answer: **Oscar Wilde was the poet and author – the year 2000 was the centenary of his death.**

Oscar Wilde was an Irishman who became one of England's most successful playwrights and poets in the late 19th century. He wrote 'The Importance of Being Earnest', 'Lady Windermere's Fan' and several other notable plays. He also wrote 'The Happy Prince' and other stories for children.

After one of the most famous English trials of the 19th century, which took place in 1895, Wilde was found guilty of 'gross indecency'. In this case it meant homosexual acts, which were illegal then, and remained so until 1967.

He was sentenced to two years hard labour in Reading Gaol where conditions were very harsh. Like other prisoners he had to work on the treadmill. But a friendly warder supplied him with Huntley & Palmer biscuits and newspapers. Wilde had been a friend of the Palmer family and had visited the Reading biscuit factory. He would undoubtedly have been able to smell the biscuits baking from his cell just across the river.

He wrote 'De Profundis' (From the Depths) while a prisoner. One of his finest works was 'The Ballad of Reading Gaol', written in France after his release.

His health never recovered from the experience of gaol and he died in 1900, aged 46. His grave in Paris receives thousands of visitors every year.

16 Kennet bank. 'Chocolate Island'.

Answer: **The figure is fishing, with rod and (imaginary) line.**

The island is known as Chocolate Island, possibly because of a connection with Huntley & Palmer's factory. Some people say they stored chocolate there for their chocolate biscuits!

17 Kennet bank. The back wall of Toys R Us.

Answer: **The cities are Bristol and Reading, which are connected by the Kennet and Avon canal.**

The Kennet and Avon Canal has an overall length of 87 miles. It is actually a combination of two lengths of navigable river linked by a canal. ('Navigable' means that boats could travel along it). Starting with the River Avon near Bristol, it is linked to the River Kennet at Newbury by canal. In all, the waterway has 105 locks from beginning to end.

The two river stretches were made navigable in the early 18th century, and the 57-mile canal section was dug between 1794 and 1810.

The Kennet and Avon played a great part in Reading's development as a market town and in the growth of the 'Three Bs' industries. By 1818, seventy 60-ton barges were working on the canal, mostly carrying coal and stone, such as the Bath Stone used to build the Royal Berks Hospital and Eldon Square. By 1832, 300,000 tons of freight were being carried each year.

Canals were favoured for carrying fragile goods, such as tiles or biscuits, and heavy, bulky loads such as stone. They were slow, but saved an enormous amount of money compared to transport by bumpy horse and cart, as they could carry huge loads by comparison.

The canal was used less and less after the railways were developed in the 1840s, but it has been restored with the help of many volunteers and was reopened in 1990. It is now used for boating, fishing, and walking and cycling the tow paths. It is also important for wildlife conservation.

18 Gas Works Road Bridge

Answer: **The company was the Reading Gas Company, 1880.**

The Reading Gas Company bought 13 acres of land from Huntley & Palmers, and in the 1880s the gas works was relocated from further along the river. Gas Works Road and the bridge were built to link the old and new works, and the road ran through the Huntley & Palmers factory site. In the late 19th century this was the heart of industrial Reading, but now it is a quiet part of town.

19 Kenavon Drive. Riverside Museum at Blake's Lock.

Answer a: **Paddles and rymers are parts of the weir construction.**

Answer b: **A weir is a barrier across a river, designed to alter its flow.**

Answer c: **The pumping station was for pumping sewage upstream in a pipe on the bed of the Kennet, to Manor**

Farm, the old sewage works in South Reading. A pumping station still operates beside the restaurant.

Weirs are man-made dams across a river. They have been used since ancient times to increase the flow of the water to drive water mills, or to act as traps for fish. The problem with them was that they made it difficult for boats to pass. That is why locks were often built alongside weirs, to enable boats to be raised safely to a higher level and move on. The earliest locks were often rather like weirs, and were called flash locks. They damned the flow of the water and raised the level, to enable a boat to float rapidly over a shallow stretch of water where it otherwise might run aground.

The River Kennet has been an important route into Reading since the 1200s, as it provides the link to the River Thames, a major waterway in Britain. The Abbot of Reading had control of the Kennet, and boats could pass through the ancient lock on payment of a penny toll to the abbey. The lock was modernised when the Kennet and Avon Canal was built, and afterwards boats could travel all the way to the Bristol area – a huge boost to trade. This lock still has manual beams, rather than hydraulic beams operated by water power.

The Riverside Museum tells the story of Reading's two rivers – the Kennet and the Thames. The museum occupies two old industrial buildings, the Screens House and the Turbine House. Exhibits include a gypsy caravan and information about the Roma people, a medieval mill wheel, preserved turbine machinery and occasionally, works of local artists

TRAIL 3: THE FORBURY AND THE ABBEY

20 Kennet bank at Kennet Mouth. Brunel Railway Bridge and Horseshoe Bridge.

Answer a: **The Horseshoe Bridge allowed horses pulling barges on the Thames to be able to cross over to the opposite tow path.**

Answer b: **The Horseshoe Bridge was built in 1891.**

Answer c: **The Railway Bridge was built in 1839-40.**

This is one of Reading's industrial heritage sites, where we can see plenty of evidence of the 19th century developments, such as the bridges, the gas works, and the brick-lined Kennet which was such an important waterway for Reading. The railway was even more important, and the river and the Great Western Railway at this point would have carried countless loads of materials into Reading, and carried biscuits, bulbs, beer and so many other products out of Reading to every corner of the world. As time went by, more and more Reading people commuted into London for work, and this old bridge has carried many millions of passengers to and from the capital. The fact that the bridge still does its job so well is a tribute to Brunel's engineering.

If you look at the face of the bridge you see drainage pipes sticking out. Sand martins are birds which fly across from Africa to nest in Britain, and some of them use these convenient pipes for nesting. At the right time of year you can see them popping in and out of the pipes.

This point, where the Rivers Kennet and Thames meet, forms a triangle of land. It is thought that some of the earliest settlements in Reading were here. The two rivers make for excellent defence,

as only one side has to be defended from attack – the land side.
The Danes built themselves an encampment here when they
took the settlement from the Saxons in 871 and fought battles
with Alfred the Great.

There is even a theory that the name 'Reading' originally meant
'the place where the waters meet in the meadow' – which might
be this spot. But more people think the name means 'Reada's
place' or 'Red's place'. Reada was possibly a Saxon chieftain.

TRAIL 4: CAVERSHAM

1   Priest Hill, Caversham. St Anne's Well.

Answer: **Pilgrims came to drink the water, which they thought had healing qualities.**

The Holy Well of St Anne is near the top of Priest Hill. Dating back to medieval times, its mineral spring waters had a reputation for healing sickness, and it was visited by pilgrims on their way to Reading Abbey. St Anne is often associated with water and rivers, and she is the patron saint of women in childbirth and of horseback riders. She was the mother of the Virgin Mary and is also known in the religion of Islam.

By the 18th century the well had been lost. It was rediscovered in 1906, and a memorial drinking fountain was built here, which was officially opened by Caversham Council in 1908.

This was at a time when Caversham was separate from the Borough of Reading, and was a village in Oxfordshire, the Thames being the county boundary. Caversham was incorporated into Reading by an Act of Parliament in 1911, which many Caversham residents did not like!

2   Church Road, Caversham. Caversham Court Gardens.

Answer a: **It was the Simonds family, famous for brewery and banking.**

Answer b: **The house was demolished in 1933, and the gardens opened in 1934.**

The gardens of what used to be Caversham Court house are now a beautiful public park. Near here, eels used to be trapped in the river, for eating. 'Buck' is an old word for a wicker basket eel trap, and we see this word in the nearby road called Buckside. The

Griffin Pub, close to the gardens, used to have rights to the eels caught here, and no doubt they served them at the pub.

The Gardens are fronting the Thames, and they originally formed part of the grounds surrounding the old Caversham Rectory, where the vicar of nearby St Peter's Church lived. The records show a house here in the 12th century, built at the same time as the Church just above the gardens. At one time the house was a home for Augustinian monks, and after the dissolution of the monasteries the property was given to Christchurch College, Oxford. Through the centuries, many notable Reading families have lived here, including the Simonds, of Simonds brewery. The Rectory was renamed Caversham Court in 1916, but was finally demolished in 1933.

In July 2007 Reading Borough Council received a £1.4 million grant from the Heritage Lottery Fund for restoration work at the Gardens, with the Council contributing £385,000.

The work included the building of an environmental pond, and repairs to the 17th-century gazebo and the 'crinkle-crankle' wall at the back of the Gardens. One of the walls has a brick with 1774 scratched on it – can you find it?

A 'crinkle-crankle', or wavy wall, is an unusual type of wall which uses fewer bricks because it can be made just one brick thick, and so is cheaper. If a wall this thin were to be made in a straight line, without supports, it would easily topple over. The curves in the wall provide stability.

Both 'crinkle' and 'crankle' are words meaning 'something with bends and turns', but the term is also thought to come from Old English meaning zig-zag.

TRAIL 4: CAVERSHAM

A gazebo is a small building, often in the garden of a fine house, used for relaxing and enjoying the view. It is not clear what language the word comes from – it may be an invented word developed from 'gaze'. Many 18th-century gardens have them, and there is a famous one in Kew Gardens. The two-storey gazebo at Caversham Court, built in the 17th century, is a very fine example. It is one of the oldest remaining gazebos in the country, and is a Grade II listed building, meaning it is protected from demolition or alteration.

3   Hemdean Road, Caversham. Information panel.

Answer a: **The creature is a swan.**

Answer b: **Old Father Time is probably the human figure, especially as he is supporting a clock. But some people think he is Old Father Thames!**

Answer c: **Some of the businesses are – Grocer's shop, photographer, a smithy making horseshoes and metal objects, a wheelwright, and a harness and saddle maker.**

Answer d: **They are called Christchurch Meadows because they used to belong to Christchurch College, Oxford. Reading Corporation bought them in 1902.**

Answer e: **Reading Town Hall, the Natural History Museum, the West Memorial Hall and the Baptist Church, were all designed by the famous architect Alfred Waterhouse. The West Memorial Hall is now housing a number of apartments, called The Waterhouse.**

Answer f: **A convoy of lorries and traction engines were**

driven across the bridge, which reassured people that the bridge was strong. It was very long for a single-span bridge, which made some people anxious about its strength.

The businesses that occupied the Church Street cottages tell us how important the horse was in everyday life before the motor car. Horses were used for the transport of people and for carrying or pulling all heavy goods. The early canal boats were pulled by horses, which is why we see tow paths on the banks of the Kennet and Avon canal, and the Kennet and Thames rivers. Even after the railways were developed, horse-drawn wagons were used to transport goods to and from the depots. Before the railway, nothing could travel faster than a horse.

The location of the Church Street cottages would have been useful for travellers, being on a crossroads and at the start of the important Caversham Bridge, which was for centuries the only bridge over the Thames at this point.

4   Caversham Bridge.

Answer a: **The building was a chapel dedicated to St Anne, the patron saint of women in childbirth.**

Answer b: **The Royalist army, led by Prince Rupert, fought against the Parliamentarians in the English Civil War.**

The River Thames has been the single most important factor in Caversham's history. Through the centuries there have been millers, boat-builders, ferrymen, eel fishers, all depending on the river here for their livelihood.

Caversham is also one of the places where some of the earliest evidence of mankind in England has been found: flints, sharpened by man, have been dug up from what was the gravel bed of the River Thames, and they are over 250,000 years old. At the time of the Domesday Book (1086) there was a permanent settlement here, then called Cavesham, so Caversham is at least as old as Reading.

5 **Thames Side Promenade, just to the west of Caversham Bridge on the Reading side of the river.**

Answer a: **The fountain was built in memory of Frank Attwells, who died in office as Mayor of Reading 1892.**

Answer b: **Dogs are not welcome on View Island.**

Answer c: **The coal yards were on land which is now part of King's Meadow.**

Frank Attwells is buried in The Old Cemetery in East Reading, where his grave is marked by an interesting memorial stone. It is a broken classical column, with a stone wreath balanced at the top.

The information board near the fountain refers to View Island and to the coal yards. The island was a derelict boatyard when Reading Borough Council took it over in 1998 and restored it. It is a quiet, relaxing island, and because wildlife is encouraged to live and breed there, dogs are not welcome as they may harm the wild creatures.

The railways carried around 165 million tons of coal each year in the late 1930s and a great deal more during the Second World War, 1939–45. Coal was the vital fuel for industry, and for generating electricity and producing gas. Nowadays, oil and natural gas produce most of our power.

Before the war, the railways used 15 million tons of coal a year to fuel the steam locomotives, and coal yards like those mentioned on the board would have been found near most British towns. The UK was very rich in coal, which is one of the reasons the Industrial Revolution took place in Britain before any other country. Today, nearly all railway trains run on diesel oil or electricity.

6   **Caversham Road, near the junction with Great Knollys Street.**

Answer: **Barberi died in the Railway Tavern in 1849. He was brought here having been taken ill on a train.**

Dominic Barberi was an Italian priest, known for having received John Henry Newman into the Catholic Church. Newman was a leading member of the Church of England, so his conversion to Catholicism caused a great deal of shock and interest. Barberi was a pioneer in getting the Catholic Church re-established in Britain in the 19th century, and so is a very well-known name among British Catholics. St James Church, next to the prison, was built in 1837 – 40, and is part of that revival of the Catholic Church in England.

The Railway Tavern became the Duke of Edinburgh pub, which closed in the 1990s. Later it was demolished and flats were built on the site.

Two Rivers Press has been publishing in and about Reading since 1994. Founded by the artist Peter Hay (1951 – 2003), the press continues to delight readers, local and further afield, with its varied list of individually designed, thought-provoking books.